The Perfect Saviour

The Perfect Saviour

Key themes in Hebrews

Peter O'Brien
Jonathan Griffiths
Richard Gaffin, Jr
David Gooding
Thomas Schreiner
Peter Walker
David Peterson
Bruce Winter

Edited by Jonathan Griffiths

ivp

INTER-VARSITY PRESS
Norton Street, Nottingham NG7 3HR, England
Website: www.ivpbooks.com
Email: ivp@ivpbooks.com

First published 2012

British Library Cataloguing in Publication Data
A catalogue record for this book is available from the British Library.

UK ISBN: 978-1-84474-583-8

Set in Monotype Garamond 11/14pt
Typeset in Great Britain by CRB Associates, Potterhanworth, Lincolnshire
Printed and bound in Great Britain by Ashford Colour Press Ltd, Gosport,
Hampshire

*Inter-Varsity Press publishes Christian books that are true to the Bible and that communicate
the gospel, develop discipleship and strengthen the church for its mission in the world.*

*Inter-Varsity Press is closely linked with the Universities and Colleges Christian Fellowship,
a student movement connecting Christian Unions in universities and colleges throughout Great
Britain, and a member movement of the International Fellowship of Evangelical Students.
Website: www.uccf.org.uk*

CONTENTS

CONTRIBUTORS

Richard B. Gaffin, Jr (ThD, Westminster Theological Seminary) is Professor Emeritus of Biblical and Systematic Theology, Westminster Theological Seminary.

David Gooding (PhD, Cambridge) is Professor Emeritus of Old Testament Greek at Queen's University Belfast and is a member of the Royal Irish Academy.

Jonathan Griffiths (PhD, Cambridge) served as Assistant Minister at Christ Church, Westbourne, and has joined the Proclamation Trust as an instructor on the Cornhill Training Course.

Peter T. O'Brien (PhD, Manchester) is Emeritus Faculty Member, formerly Vice-Principal and Senior Research Fellow in New Testament, Moore College, Sydney.

David Peterson (PhD, Manchester) served as Principal of Oak Hill Theological College, London, and is now Emeritus Faculty Member at Moore College, Sydney.

Thomas R. Schreiner (PhD, Fuller Theological Seminary) is the James Buchanan Harrison Professor of New Testament Interpretation at Southern Baptist Theological Seminary.

Peter Walker (PhD, Cambridge and DPhil, Oxford) is Associate Vice-Principal and Tutor in New Testament and Biblical Theology at Wycliffe Hall, Oxford.

Bruce W. Winter (PhD, Macquarie) is Director of the Institute for Early Christianity in the Graeco-Roman World, Emmanuel College, University of Queensland, Brisbane, Senior Research Fellow in Ancient History, Macquarie University, Sydney and Visiting Fellow, St Edmund's College, University of Cambridge 2007–12.

ABBREVIATIONS

AB	Anchor Bible
CBQ	*Catholic Biblical Quarterly*
EDNT	*Exegetical Dictionary of the New Testament*, ed. H. Balz and G. Schneider, 3 vols. (ET, Grand Rapids, 1990–93)
ESV	English Standard Version
KJV	King James Version
JBL	*Journal of Biblical Literature*
JRS	*Journal of Roman Studies*
JSNT	*Journal for the Study of the New Testament*
JSNTSS	Journal for the Study of the New Testament Supplement Series
LS	*A Greek-English Lexicon*, H. G. Liddell and R. Scott, (Oxford, ^{8}1897)
LXX	Septuagint
NASB	New American Standard Bible
NDBT	*New Dictionary of Biblical Theology*, ed. T. Desmond Alexander and Brian S. Rosner (Leicester, 2000)
NEB	New English Bible
NICNT	New International Commentary on the New Testament

NIV	New International Version
NKJV	New King James Version
NRSV	New Revised Standard Version
NSBT	New Studies in Biblical Theology
NTS	*New Testament Studies*
PNTC	Pillar New Testament Commentary
RSV	Revised Standard Version
RV	Revised Version
SNTSMS	Society for New Testament Studies Monograph Series
TDNT	*Theological Dictionary of the New Testament*, ed. G. Kittel and G. Friedrich, tr. G. W. Bromiley, 10 vols. (Grand Rapids, 1964–76)
TJ	*Trinity Journal*
TNIV	Today's New International Version
TynB	*Tyndale Bulletin*
WBC	Word Biblical Commentary
WUNT	Wissenschaftliche Untersuchungen zum Neuen Testament

PREFACE

When I was studying theology, each week my tutors (one of whom has written a chapter in this volume) would set an essay title and a reading list covering a major theme in a New Testament book. We students would go away, read up on that theme, reflect on it for a week, and write three or four thousand words on it. For each New Testament book that we studied, we only had opportunity to write four or five essays, but at the end of that series of detailed studies on key themes, we came to see that we had four or five solid footholds to equip us to tackle the book and to know it well. Gaining a firm grasp of a few key issues within a book was, for me, the best way of getting to know the book as a whole.

This present volume is, if you like, a tutorial series on the book of Hebrews. It is designed to help preachers embarking on a sermon series to get their heads around Hebrews – its key themes and difficult questions. This is not a full theology of Hebrews, but a theological taster and introduction, designed primarily for pastors. It is hoped that it will be of value to those leading Bible study groups and those in theological education as well.

The impetus for this project came from a desire to bridge the gap between the work being done on Hebrews by evangelical scholars in universities and colleges and the real world of the busy preacher.

Too often good New Testament research never makes it to the pastor's study because it is presented in a form that is not practically digestible in the time that a pastor has for sermon preparation. And if you are reading this now, I imagine that you will share the conviction of the authors that theological research is only valuable insofar as it aids the proclamation of the gospel.

The idea for this volume took shape in my mind as I studied the work that David Peterson did for his PhD on the theme of perfection in Hebrews. This is an important theme and David's study is excellent. But many pastors will not have time or opportunity to read the monograph that David produced as a result of that study. When I suggested this present project and asked David if he would produce a précis of his research, he kindly agreed, and the project was born. I owe him very special thanks.

I must also register my gratitude to all the contributors and to Philip Duce at Inter-Varsity Press for their willingness to invest time and energy into this project. I know that they share my prayer that it will be for the good of the church and the glory of her Lord.

Jonathan Griffiths

1. THE NEW COVENANT AND ITS PERFECT MEDIATOR

Peter T. O'Brien

Within the New Testament the most developed theology of the new covenant is found in the letter to the Hebrews. Important covenantal imagery appears throughout this 'word of exhortation' (Heb. 13:22) as the writer returns to the subject repeatedly. The significant theological term *diathēkē* ('covenant') turns up seventeen times (7:22; 8:6, 8, 9 [twice], 10; 9:4 [twice], 15 [twice], 16, 17, 20; 10:16, 29; 12:24; 13:20), in addition to six other instances where the noun is understood (8:7 [twice], 13 [twice]; 9:1, 18) – making a total of twenty-three occurrences.[1] Most of these fall within the central theological section of the letter (though note 10:29; 12:24; 13:20)[2] where the author

---

1. S. Lehne, *The New Covenant in Hebrews,* JSNTSS 44 (Sheffield: JSOT Press, 1990), pp. 11–12.
2. Heb. 10:29 and 13:20 appear in exhortatory material (10:26–39; 13:1–25). Heb. 12:24 is part of the exposition ('You have come to Mount Zion', 12:18–24) that summarizes the main points and theological themes of the letter. Each of these instances of the term 'covenant' picks up earlier foundational statements.

employs the new covenant text of Jeremiah 31:31–34 as an *inclusio* (Heb. 8:8–12; 10:16–17). After dealing with the Son's appointment as the unique high priest (5:1 – 7:28), in which the author highlights the superiority of the new covenant (7:22), he then proceeds to elaborate on this in chapters 8 – 10, particularly in relation to the superiority of Christ's new covenant sacrifice. The cultic argument of these three chapters is set within the context of a discussion of covenant.

Although God made covenants with Noah (Gen. 6:18; 9:9–17), Abraham (Gen. 15:18; 17:1–14), Isaac (Gen. 17:19–21), Jacob (Exod. 2:24; 6:4), Israel at Sinai (Exod. 24:3–8), and the dynasty of David (2 Sam. 7), Hebrews, rather surprisingly, uses the term *diathēkē* only of the Sinai covenant (Exod. 24:3–8) and the new covenant promised in Jeremiah 31:31–34. This may be explained in part by our author's focus on and detailed discussion of the relationships between the Mosaic system and the new covenant. At the same time, we need to account for Hebrews' wide-ranging use of the language of promise throughout the discourse, and thus how promises and covenants relate to one another.

Promises and covenants

These two important motifs of promise and covenant are closely connected. In Hebrews terms for 'promise' refer to God's commitments to his people. His making a promise points to his giving a pledge or gift or assurance that he will perform some action, usually of a positive kind.[3] 'Promise' can refer to the word or pledge initially given, or the substance of the thing promised when God fulfils his commitment (Heb. 6:12, 17; 9:15; 11:8–9). For the author of Hebrews the fundamental promises are those made to Abraham, and include God's pledge to bless him, and to give him land and

---

3. Craig R. Koester, *Hebrews: A New Translation with Introduction and Commentary*, AB 36 (New York: Doubleday, 2001), p. 110.

descendants (6:14; 11:9, 12). These promises, which express commitments that remain in force for all of Abraham's heirs, including the followers of Jesus, indicate the goal or purpose of God's overall plan.[4]

Covenants provide the *means* or mechanism for achieving the divine intention. A 'covenant' is a binding agreement that establishes the basis for interaction between its parties. In Hebrews, covenant language is not about a mutual agreement, contract or negotiation which needs an arbiter. Instead, the covenant is a gracious gift from God. So Jesus' role as *mediator* is not in a strict sense that of an arbiter or intermediary of a bilateral agreement. The terms of the covenant are not in dispute or up for discussion, as though Jesus had to act as mediator by bringing the two parties together to hammer out an agreement. He is an agent, or delegate, invested with divine authority in God's settlement, which Jesus realizes and guarantees.

God's promises provide the basis for both the old and new covenants (Heb. 8:6). The first covenant was established on the promise that Israel would be God's people (Exod. 6:7; 29:45; Lev. 26:12), while the *better* promises on which the new covenant is based appear in the quotation from Jeremiah 31:31–34, and (while building on the reality of God's people), include God's implanting his laws in their hearts (Heb. 8:10), which implies receiving a new heart (Ezek. 11:19–20; 36:26–27), the knowledge of God as a matter of personal experience (Heb. 8:11), and an announcement within the new covenant itself that the Lord will forgive his people's sins (Heb. 8:12). In both covenants, then, God's word of promise precedes the 'mechanism', that is, the covenant, by which the promise is put into effect.

We turn next to the new covenant oracle of Jeremiah 31:31–34 which the author cites in full at a pivotal point in his discourse.

---

4. Lehne, *New Covenant*, p. 20, rightly points out that God's promises span the ages, from Abraham (6:13) to the time when the very heavens will be shaken (12:26).

The new covenant of Jeremiah 31

In the longest single quotation of the Old Testament in the New, the author of Hebrews cites the classic new covenant passage of Jeremiah 31:31–34 (Heb. 8:8–12) to introduce an important section of Hebrews' central theological argument (8:7 – 10:18). At the conclusion of this exposition (10:15–17) Jeremiah 31 is cited again, this time in an abbreviated form. The two respective quotations function as bookends to frame the whole section, which speaks of the nature of the new covenant that Jesus mediates (8:7–13), and the new covenant offering which his high priestly ministry includes (9:1 – 10:18). Against the backdrop of the Old Testament priestly sacrificial system 'Hebrews presents a sustained, expositional argument that identifies Jesus as the superior, heavenly high priest, the mediator of a new and better covenant'.[5]

The divine initiative and a fresh unfolding of God's redemptive purpose

The author's introductory and concluding remarks (8:7–8a, 13) that frame the Jeremiah 31 citation underscore the imperfect and provisional nature of the old covenant that God made with Israel at Sinai. While the nation's disobedience and failure to keep the covenant demands were a major issue (8:9), had it been the only problem with the first covenant, God might have renewed the people's willingness to obey it. But by replacing it with a new one, he showed that the first covenant was flawed and brought nothing to perfection or completion (7:11, 19). A new unfolding of God's redemptive purpose had taken place, and this called for a new covenant action on God's part. He declared that the Sinai covenant

5. C. C. Newman, 'Covenant, new covenant', in *Dictionary of the Later New Testament and Its Developments*, eds. R. P. Martin and P. H. Davids (Downers Grove and Leicester: IVP, 1997), pp. 245–250, esp. p. 248.

was unserviceable and outmoded; it had passed its 'use by' date, and its demise was a foregone conclusion (8:13).[6]

God took the initiative in announcing his intention to establish a new covenant. Throughout the oracle of Jeremiah 31 the dominant use of the first person emphatically underlines the divine initiative: 'I will make . . . I will write . . . I will be . . . I will be merciful . . . I will remember . . . ' (Heb. 8:8–12). The prophecy itself is punctuated by the phrase, 'declares the Lord' (vv. 8, 9; 10, cf. 10:16).

This fresh unfolding of God's purposes is to occur when 'the days are coming' (8:8), a common prophetic phrase in Jeremiah (7:32; 9:25, etc.). It recalls the opening of Hebrews where God spoke 'in *these* last days' (1:2), and the implication is that the time announced by Jeremiah has arrived – the time of climactic fulfilment. The assured success of the new covenant is implied by the author's choice of language, namely, that God will *complete* or consummate (*synteleō*) a covenant with his people (rather than simply 'make' or 'establish') it. This echoes other words for *completion* in Hebrews (2:10; 5:9; 7:28), and recalls the theme of Christ's perfection.

The marks of the new covenant

The characteristics of the new covenant promised by Jeremiah that the Lord initiates between himself and his people are threefold.

God's law implanted in his people's hearts

> I will put my laws into their minds,
>> and write them on their hearts (Heb. 8:10; cf. 10:16).

---

6. For a criticism of the view that the oracle of Jer. 31:31–34 has only a negative function in Hebrews, while in Jeremiah it functions both negatively and positively, see the discussion and relevant literature in P. T. O'Brien, *The Letter to the Hebrews*, PNTC (Grand Rapids: Eerdmans; Nottingham: Apollos, 2010), pp. 294–295.

This means much more than committing the law to memory (Deut.
6:6–9), which did not guarantee the performance of what had been
remembered. Israel, by turning aside to its own ways again and again,
showed this throughout its history. Jeremiah recognized that the
hearts of the people were engraved with sin, not with the law (Jer.
17:1). But in the new covenant there is a fundamental difference
from the old: the Lord himself will write his law on the hearts of
his people. Thus, obedience from the heart, which was expected
under the old covenant (Deut. 26:16; 28:45–47; 1 Kgs 3:6), will now
be accomplished by God. Also, this writing is not in the hearts of
'scattered individuals' but of the people as a whole; it is not simply
internal but also universal (cf. Heb. 8:11, 'they shall *all* know me,
from the least of them to the greatest'). Jeremiah's words imply the
people's receiving of a new heart, which is expressly promised in
the parallel prophecy of Ezekiel: 'I will give them one heart, and a
new spirit I will put within them. I will remove the heart of stone
from their flesh and give them a heart of flesh, that they may walk
in my statutes and keep my rules and obey them' (Ezek. 11:19–20;
36:26–27).

If this covenant was new in relation to God's writing his law in
their hearts (or giving them a new heart), then the covenant
formula, which underscores the uniqueness of the relationship,
remains unchanged: 'I will be their God, and they shall be
my people' (Heb. 8:10). This formula was the substance of the
covenant of Moses' day (Exod. 6:7; 29:45; Lev. 26:12). It was reiter-
ated as a promise throughout the rest of the Old Testament (Jer.
7:23; Hos. 2:23; Zech. 8:8), taken up and applied in apostolic days
to the people of the new covenant (2 Cor. 6:16), and repeated in
the New Testament Apocalypse when the new heaven and earth
come into being (Rev. 21:3, 'Behold, the dwelling place of God is
with man. He will dwell with them, and they will be his people, and
God himself will be with them as their God'). Although the
covenant slogan remained the same throughout salvation history,
'I will be their God' was filled with fresh meaning with every
unfolding revelation of his character, while 'you will be my

people' acquired deeper significance as his will was more fully known by them.[7]

The knowledge of God as a matter of personal experience

[T]hey shall not teach, each one his neighbour
> and each one his brother, saying, 'Know the Lord,'
for they shall all know me,
> from the least of them to the greatest (Heb. 8:11).

At one level the people of Israel knew their God, because he had revealed himself to them, in contrast with the surrounding nations which did not know him. But Hebrews recalls that the works performed for Moses' generation (Heb. 3:9; Ps. 95) which displayed his power, did not lead to the people knowing his ways (Heb. 3:10). After the generation that entered Canaan under Joshua died out, the following generation 'did not know the LORD' (Judg. 2:10). Later Hosea complained that there was no 'knowledge of God in the land' (Hos. 4:1, 6). Jeremiah's prophecy envisages not simply a national knowledge of God, but a personal knowledge of him, such as Jeremiah himself possessed. God promised that every member of the covenant community would know him directly and personally, 'from the least of them to the greatest' – the result of his writing his laws on each heart or, as Ezekiel put it, because each would be given a new heart and spirit by God. The expression, 'they shall not teach, each one his neighbour', is not a rejection of teaching or leadership but a powerful affirmation of the universality of this unmediated knowledge of God. The emphatic words, 'they shall all know me', demonstrate this. To know God is to recognize him, to trust him, and to obey him. Every believer is able to approach God in a personal and direct way 'with confidence' because Jesus has made this possible through his high-priestly work (4:16; 7:25;

---

7. F. F. Bruce, *The Epistle to the Hebrews*, NICNT (rev. ed., Grand Rapids: Eerdmans, 1990), p. 71.

10:19–22; 12:22–24). Such intimate knowledge increases until it reaches its consummation, when all of us will know fully as we are fully known.

The Lord will forgive his people's sins
The climax of the quotation, which is repeated in an expanded form in Hebrews 10:17, is the announcement in the new covenant:

> For I will be merciful toward their iniquities,
> And I will remember their sins no more (Heb. 8:12).

The introductory 'for' shows that the basis of the preceding promises is the assurance of a decisive cleansing from sin. For the author of Hebrews this definitive forgiveness of sins is foundational to the new covenant. The forgiveness of sins was known and experienced in the Old Testament (Exod. 34:6–7; Mic. 7:18–19; Ps. 51; Neh. 9:26–31) as believers cast themselves upon God and pleaded for his mercy, as David did after his adultery with Bathsheba and murder of Uriah the Hittite (Ps. 51; see 2 Sam. 11 – 12). However, for David (or any other Israelite) there was no provision for the forgiveness of sins of a high hand *under the old covenant*. The penalty would be death by stoning. In fact, under the old sacrificial system there was an annual reminder of sins (Heb. 10:3). But under the new covenant no such calling of sins to mind operates, for God says that he will remember their sins no more. Because of Christ's sacrifice offered once for all on the cross (7:27) God in his grace forgives them.

The new covenant – renewal or replacement?
Because of the similarities between the two covenants and the fact that the covenant formula ('I will be their God, and they shall be my people', 8:10) remains unchanged, many regard the new covenant as a 'renewal' of the old rather than its replacement. But while both covenants were based on divine promises, those on which the new covenant was established were better (8:6). Moreover, Hebrews draws attention to a number of fundamental differences between

the two covenants: first, a profound weakness of the old covenant is that neither it nor the priesthood associated with it could attain 'perfection' (7:11, 19). As a result, the disobedience of the people with whom the first covenant was made (8:9) showed a fundamental weakness in it (8:7). Second, and directly related to this, the covenants differ significantly in their ability to deal with sin. Christ's sacrifice of himself cleanses the consciences of his people so that they may serve the living God (9:14; 10:16–18). By Christ's perfecting work the 'perfection' of his people is able to be realized. The Levitical sacrifices could only remind the people of their sin (10:1–4), while the Day of Atonement ritual in the old covenant (Lev. 16) 'enables Hebrews to present Christ's death as the sacrifice that fulfils the *new covenant*'.[8] Unlike the old covenant, the new cannot be broken. 'Sin cannot imperil the divine-human relationships guaranteed by this new covenant, for sin will not be brought into account: "God will forgive their wickedness and will remember their sins no more".'[9] For these reasons, one must conclude that the new covenant is radically *new*. And with the fulfilment of its divine promises new meaning is given to the covenant formula, 'I will be their God, and they shall be my people'.

Christ and the new covenant

We have already seen that the new covenant is intimately related to Christ and his work. He is its 'mediator' (*mesitēs*; 8:6; 9:15; 12:24), as well as the 'guarantor' or 'surety' (*engyos*; 7:22) of this covenant, which is described in Hebrews as 'second' (8:7), 'new' (8:8; 9:15; 12:24), 'better' (7:22; 8:6) and 'eternal' (13:20). As 'mediator' of the new covenant Christ is involved in its establishment. A 'surety' or

---

8. Koester, *Hebrews*, p. 390, emphasis original.
9. P. R. Williamson, *Sealed With an Oath: Covenant in God's Unfolding Purpose*, NSBT 23 (Nottingham: Apollos, 2007), p. 157; cf. P. R. Williamson, 'Covenant', in *NDBT*, pp. 419–429.

'guarantor' (*engyos* was commonly used in Hellenistic Greek) was a person who assumed responsibility for another's debt if the latter could not meet it. As 'guarantor' of the new covenant (7:22) Christ is its pledge who secures its ultimate success.

While the marks of the new covenant were presented in Hebrews 8 in the citation of Jeremiah 31:31–34, how the covenant was to be established and the means by which the promised forgiveness of sins (8:12) was to be effected are not explained until Hebrews 9 – 10. Thus, the full significance of Jeremiah's oracle (31:31–34) can be understood only in the light of Christ's sacrifice, and the positive counterpart does not appear until after the specific reference is made to this in Hebrews 9:11–14, when the author speaks explicitly of Christ's relation to the new covenant (9:15). Here the Day of Atonement ritual is employed typologically of Christ's sacrifice and exaltation, and provides the basis for the important conclusion of verse 15, that Jesus' costly sacrifice has inaugurated the new covenant and he has become its 'mediator'.

The superiority of Christ's sacrifice to the offerings under the old covenant is established on the grounds that: (a) the *place* of his offering was in heaven rather than on earth (9:11, 23–25; 10:12–13); (b) the *blood* of his sacrifice was his own rather than that of animals (9:12–28); and (c) the offering of the heavenly high priest was *eternal*: it was made once for all, and is therefore unlike the continuous sacrifices of the Levitical priests (9:25–26; 10:1–18).[10]

He who was the sinless high priest (4:15; 7:26) was also the spotless victim. His action in offering himself through the eternal Spirit to God as an unblemished sacrifice accomplished a decisive cleansing of the conscience (9:14). At the point where a man or

---

10. G. H. Guthrie, *Hebrews: The NIV Application Commentary* (Grand Rapids: Zondervan, 1998), p. 297. On the view that *diathēkē* refers to the broken Sinai 'covenant' rather than 'testament' in Heb. 9:16–17, see Williamson, *Sealed*, pp. 203–206; S. W. Hahn, *Kinship by Covenant: A Canonical Approach to the Fulfillment of God's Saving Promises* (New Haven: Yale University Press, 2009), pp. 307–320; and O'Brien, *Hebrews*, pp. 328–332.

woman confronts the holiness of God with a guilty conscience, there Christ's propitiatory sacrifice effects a definitive cleansing from the practices and attitudes that belong to the way of death, and turns aside God's righteous wrath from sinners. Freed from this dreadful bondage men and women can now serve and worship the living God in spirit and truth as he intended (9:14).

Christ's death as a sacrifice consummated the old order. According to Hebrews, his death 'redeems them from the transgressions committed under the first covenant' (9:15). His sacrifice was the price of deliverance from judgment and guilt that resulted from sin. The 'first covenant' exacted death for transgressions committed under it. Those who pledged their obedience to it and subsequently transgressed failed to keep their promises and were in danger of being cut off from God (Deut. 30:15–20). Jesus identified with the transgressors and died a representative death for them. His redemptive sacrifice is retrospective in its effects and is valid for all who trusted God for the forgiveness of sins in ancient Israel (see 11:40).

Moreover, Jesus' death inaugurated the new order. The old covenant promised the land of Canaan as an inheritance for God's people. The divine purpose in Jesus' becoming the mediator of the new covenant is that 'those who are called may receive the promised eternal inheritance' (9:15). The new covenant oracle of Hebrews 8:8–12 made no mention of inheritance, although the listeners understood themselves to be *heirs* of the promises made to Abraham (2:16; 6:12–18; 11:8), who have a hope of *inheriting* salvation in the world to come (1:14). Now, however, in 9:15 the new covenant is connected with the motif of inheritance. Jesus is the mediator of this covenant through his sacrificial death, and God's purpose is that his people might receive the *eternal inheritance* – not simply the *promise* of the eternal inheritance but the inheritance *itself* – at the consummation.

The author of Hebrews concludes his lengthy treatment of Christ's superior priesthood and his new covenant offering (5:1 – 10:18) with a resounding climax (10:15–18): the Holy Spirit provides *ongoing* testimony through the new covenant prophecy of Jeremiah 31 to the author of Hebrews and his readers directly ('us', 10:15), and ultimately to other believers as well, that Christ's sacrifice provides a definitive cleansing of the conscience (10:17–18) and a resulting obedience of the heart which is expressed in positive consecration to God (10:16). God's promises have been wonderfully fulfilled. What was a future expectation from the time of Jeremiah has become a present reality because of Christ's atoning death on the cross.

The final reference in the letter to Jesus in relation to the new covenant occurs in the concluding doxology of Hebrews where it is stated that God brought back the Lord Jesus from the dead 'by the blood of the eternal covenant' (13:20). In this concentrated phrase, the author 'rehearses in an extremely condensed way, the exposition of Christ's sacrificial act'.[11] 'Blood' refers to his sacrificial death (9:12, 14; 10:19; 12:24; 13:12), and specifically in relation to the new covenant (9:20; 10:29). This is the only time in Hebrews that the covenant is called 'eternal', but the notion of eternal reality has been prominent throughout the discourse (1:8; 5:6, 9; 6:20; 9:12, 14, 15, etc.). Further, our author has repeatedly underscored the transitory nature of the old covenant (cf. 8:13), and the permanent nature of Christ's work (9:25–28; 10:12–13), which is linked with the new covenant (9:14–15). Hebrews uses the adjective 'eternal' in relation to salvation (5:9), judgment (6:2), redemption (9:12), the Spirit (9:14) and inheritance (9:15), all of which are intimately related to the new covenant.

God's powerful intervention in bringing the Lord Jesus back from the dead recalls the wording of Isaiah 63:11 (LXX) in which there is an allusion to Moses and the exodus. God 'brought up out of the sea, the shepherds of the sheep', that is, Moses and his people (Isa. 63:12–14). God's 'leading out' his people is his fundamental redemptive action under both old and new covenants. This intervention in

---

11. H. W. Attridge, *The Epistle to the Hebrews: A Commentary on the Epistle to the Hebrews*, Hermeneia (Philadelphia: Fortress, 1989), p. 406.

leading his people from Egypt recorded in the Torah and the prophets, and from the realm of the dead in the Psalter, prefigured his decisive action in raising Jesus from the dead.[12] Further, this action of God anticipates the way he will bring many sons and daughters to glory (2:10).

The idea that God brought back the Lord Jesus from the dead '*through* the blood of the eternal covenant' has been taken by recent commentators and translations as 'by' or 'through',[13] in the sense that the resurrection of Jesus occurred by virtue of the sprinkling of his blood in the heavenly sanctuary and the establishment of the new covenant.[14] Bruce agrees that Jesus was brought up from death 'by the blood of the eternal covenant', and thinks it means that Christ's 'resurrection is the demonstration that his sacrifice of himself has been accepted by God and the new covenant established on the basis of that sacrifice'.[15]

By using this metaphor at the conclusion of his letter our author highlights the work of the crucified and exalted Lord Jesus as the 'great Shepherd' who cares for and provides security for his flock.

The people of the new covenant

The beneficiaries of the new covenant are clearly those in whom the promises of Jeremiah 31:31–34 find their fulfilment. They are, therefore, those in whose hearts God has implanted his laws (Heb. 8:10), for whom the knowledge of God is a matter of personal experience (8:11) and whose sins the Lord has forgiven (8:12). They

---

12. W. L. Lane, *Hebrews*, WBC 47, 2 vols. (Dallas: Word, 1991), vol. 2, p. 561.

13. So the NRSV, REB, NIV, TNIV, ESV; the TEV has 'as the result of his sacrificial death'.

14. Lane, *Hebrews*, vol. 2, pp. 559, 563. Others suggest the phrase has the notion of accompaniment or attendant circumstances.

15. Bruce, *Hebrews*, p. 388.

are his people and he is their God (8:10). These promises are for
God's people as a whole, not simply scattered individuals, for all will
know him, from the least to the greatest (8:10–12).[16]

A wide range of designations

The letter to the Hebrews uses a wide range of terms to refer to the
members of the new covenant community. We briefly note some
of these designations in the opening chapters of the discourse
before turning to Hebrews 8 – 10 where covenant language is
concentrated.

Jesus fulfils God's design for creation and displays what had
always been intended for humankind (Ps. 8; Heb. 2:5–9). The glory
that God's sons and daughters have as their destiny (2:10) is that
which the Son had from all eternity (1:3), and with which he was
crowned at his exaltation (2:7–9). The divine purposes for the whole
of humanity, picked up from Psalm 8 (Heb. 2:5–9), find their fulfilment in the Son and those who belong to him.

This community comprises the 'many sons and daughters' (*pollous
huious*) whom God, in his gracious overarching purposes, is bringing
'to glory' by making Jesus 'the founder of their salvation perfect
through suffering' (2:10). They are God's people who have been
'sanctified' (or 'made holy', a covenantal term, 9:13–14; see below)
by the Son. He and they share their origin in God (2:11): Christ was
uniquely the Son of God (1:2, 5), others are sons (and daughters)
of God in an extended sense (2:10). Christ is not ashamed to call
them his 'brothers [and sisters]' (2:11) or to declare God's name
to them in the assembly of his people (*ekklēsia*, 2:12; note 12:23),
for they are the children whom God has given to him (2:13). The
Son shared their human nature, so that through his death he might

---

16. See further P. Gräbe, 'The New Covenant and Christian Identity in
    Hebrews', in R. Bauckham, D. Driver, T. Hart and N. MacDonald
    (eds.), *A Cloud of Witnesses: The Theology of Hebrews in its Ancient Contexts*,
    Library of New Testament Studies 387 (London: T. & T. Clark, 2008),
    pp. 118–127.

be victorious over the great adversary who has the power of death, that is, the devil, and might liberate his prisoners from their fear of death (2:14–15). They are 'the offspring of Abraham' whom Christ has taken firm hold of (*epilambanomai*, 2:16). In Hebrews this designation speaks not only of Israel's ancestors but also of the Christian community, that is, believing Jews and Gentiles (Heb. 11:39–40; Gal. 3:29; Rom. 4:13, 16), the numerous descendants promised to Abraham, and 'heirs of the promise' (6:13–17) which is embodied in the new covenant (8:6).

This covenant community is called '*the people*' (*laos*) who are the beneficiaries of Jesus' high priestly ministry (4:9; 7:27; 8:10; 10:30; 13:12). For them he became 'a merciful and faithful high priest in the service of God' in order 'to make propitiation for the sins of *the people*' (2:17–18). This involved restoring a relationship marred by sin and encompasses both expiation (sin's removal) and propitiation (the averting of divine wrath).[17]

God's people are described in Hebrews 3 by means of family imagery: the listeners are addressed directly as 'brothers [and sisters]' (3:1; 2:12), who belong to God's household (2:11–12; 3:1, 6), and can be called 'holy' because they have been sanctified by Christ (2:11; 10:10, 14). They have become *sharers* in a 'heavenly calling' (3:1; cf. Phil. 3:14; 2 Tim. 1:9), a description which tells us not only that God summoned them from heaven (through the preaching of the gospel), but also that the goal of this calling is heaven itself, where Christ himself has been exalted (1:3; 4:15; 7:26) and is presently active on their behalf (2:17–18; 7:25; 9:24). They and, by implication, other believers, are also *sharers* 'in Christ' (3:14), which could mean that Christians (share with one another) in Christ himself as part of his house (3:6). But the phrase probably signifies that they are sharers *in* Christ: as companions of the Son of God they share his joy (1:9) and participate in his inheritance (1:14). Their hope is of sharing with him in the glory attained through his death and exaltation

---

17. For a discussion and further references, see O'Brien, *Hebrews*, pp. 118–124.

(2:8–9), and so of participating in his heavenly and unshakable kingdom (12:28).

However, when the author speaks of the listeners' membership in God's household (3:6) and of their sharing in Christ (3:14), he points out that their continuance is dependent on their holding firmly to the end. In each reference a conditional sentence is introduced: we are God's house '*if indeed* we hold fast our confidence and our boasting in our hope' (3:6); and we have come to share in Christ '*if indeed* we hold our original confidence firm to the end' (3:14). As the author addresses his listeners (and includes himself, *we*), he declares that Christ's partners or members of God's household have God's promise of an inheritance in the world to come (1:2, 14). Their initial resolve and assurance, when they first welcomed the gospel into their lives, were grounded in the divine promise. But since continuance is the test of the reality of their faith, let them persevere until the final day and show that it is truly genuine (note the many references to endurance and perseverance: 4:1, 3, 11; 6:11–12; 10:36; 12:1–2, etc.).

Sanctification, perfection and definitive cleansing

In Hebrews 8 – 10, where there is a concentration of new covenant language in relation to Christ's sacrifice, the recipients of the new covenant promises are spoken of as 'sanctified' or 'made holy' (cf. 10:10, 14), 'perfected', and as those whose consciences have been cleansed (9:14; see above). While there is a significantly close relationship between sanctification, perfection and cleansing from sin in Hebrews, they are not synonymous.

The sanctification of God's people was the goal of Christ's fulfilling the Father's will by offering himself as a sacrifice for sins (10:10). The designation of believers as already 'sanctified' is consistent with the stress on sanctification as something that has already been won for us by the blood of Christ. So the description, 'we have been sanctified' (10:10), signifies a *definitive* consecration to God through the effective cleansing from sin (2:11; 9:13–14; 10:10, 29; 13:12) that qualifies us for fellowship with him. Bruce aptly remarks: 'The sanctification which his people receive in consequence is their inward cleansing from sin and their being made fit for the presence of God, so that henceforth they can offer him acceptable worship.'[18] Accordingly, we 'can draw near to God *now* with the directness and certainty that belong to the final state of his people'[19] (cf. 4:16; 10:19–22; 12:22–24). The language of approaching or drawing near to God is thus used by the author to speak of the privilege won by Christ for the new covenant people (4:16; 7:19, 25; 10:19–22; 11:6; cf. 6:19).

But 'our sanctification or consecration to God is only part of the process of eschatological perfection, achieved through the perfecting of Christ' (2:10; 5:9; 7:28).[20] The terminology of 'perfection' emphasizes the realized aspect of salvation as well as the permanent effects for believers. The context of Hebrews 10:14 locates this perfecting in the past, since it was accomplished by Christ's single offering of himself by which he perfected his people 'for all time' (10:14). At the same time, however, perfection is used 'to proclaim the fulfilment or *consummation* of men and women in a permanent, direct and personal relationship to God'.[21] Christ's death secures for believers a share in the future that God has promised. The perfection of believers involves all of this. So 'perfection' language is used of the 'complete realization at the final fulfilment of all God's promises (11:40; 12:23), ... an unfolding of what is, in principle, even now achieved through Christ's sacrifice'.[22]

Promises and warnings for the new covenant people
Those who belong to the people of God (his 'many sons and daughters', Christ's 'brothers and sisters', 'Abraham's children', etc.) must hold unswervingly to the hope they profess in obedience to

18. Bruce, *Hebrews*, p. 243.
19. D. G. Peterson, *Possessed by God: A New Testament Theology of Sanctification and Holiness*, NSBT 1 (Leicester: Apollos, 1995), p. 36.
20. Peterson, *Possessed*, pp. 36–37.
21. Ibid., p. 36, emphasis original.
22. D. G. Peterson, *Hebrews and Perfection: An Examination of the Concept of Perfection in the 'Epistle to the Hebrews'*, SNTSMS 47 (Cambridge: Cambridge University Press, 1982), p. 152.

the word of God and on the basis of their new covenant relationship with the Son. Through divine promises, encouraging words,
stern warnings, as well as positive and negative examples, the author
of Hebrews hammers home repeatedly the importance of faithful
endurance in order to reach their eternal rest in the heavenly city.
The listeners are urged to 'run with endurance the race that is set
before us, looking to Jesus, the founder and perfecter of our faith'
(12:1–2). In stark contrast, those who refuse to listen to the one who
warns from heaven will face a fearful expectation of judgment
(10:27–30; 12:25).

The exhortatory material that immediately follows the theological
section in which most of Hebrews' covenant references appear
(i.e., 8:1 – 10:18) contains an encouragement (10:19–25) and a stern
warning (10:26–31) for the listeners. Each of these exhortatory
sections is *based on* and an *application of* the author's teaching about
Christ's new covenant sacrifice. The two exhortations 'let us draw
near' (10:22), and 'let us hold fast the confession of our hope without
wavering' (10:23) are grounded in the *present* possessions of
Christians: 'since we *have* confidence to enter the holy places by the
blood of Jesus' (10:19), 'since we *have* a great priest over the house
of God' (10:21), and 'with our hearts sprinkled clean from an evil
conscience' (10:22).

Similarly, the stern warning of 10:26–31 draws out the implications, in this case negative, for those who wilfully and continuously
reject the Son of God and his new covenant sacrifice (8:1 – 10:18).
If through the gospel, people have received 'the knowledge of the
truth' and then deliberately and persistently keep on sinning so that
they turn their backs on Christ's redemptive death, then 'there no
longer remains a sacrifice for sins' (10:26). It cannot be otherwise.
Christ by his single, perfect sacrifice has provided complete cleansing
for sins and put an end to other sacrifices (9:26; 10:18). If this way
of forgiveness and acceptance with God is utterly and finally rejected,
all hope of salvation is lost. The shocking nature of apostasy under
the new covenant describes a persistent attitude (10:29) in which a
person: (a) tramples the Son of God underfoot, (b) rejects Christ's

new covenant sacrifice, the very means by which God has claimed his people for himself, and (c) arrogantly insults the Holy Spirit of God who was active in the Son's work on the cross (9:14) and in the initial preaching of the gospel of grace (2:3–4; 6:4–6).

Although the author of Hebrews does not say that members of the congregation have actually committed apostasy, he is clearly concerned that some may be in great danger of falling over this precipice. Those who reject the blessings of the new covenant are deserving of far greater punishment, namely, spiritual death (10:29), than what the Mosaic law prescribed, which was physical death.[23] The strong language of judgment in 10:27–31 echoes the divine judgment mentioned within the covenantal context of Deuteronomy: it has affinities with the covenantal curses of Deuteronomy 28 – 29 (Heb. 10:27, 31, 'fearful'), and is confirmed by a twofold appeal to the Song of Moses (Deut. 32; Heb. 10:30) in which the Lord assumes personal responsibility for judging those who have become his adversaries (Deut. 32:35–36).

In conclusion, those who lay hold of God's promises and words of encouragement, heed the strong warnings, and persevere faithfully to the end, show that their enduring faith is genuine. They are true members of the new covenant people who will reach their eternal rest in the heavenly city. But those who despise the Son of God and utterly reject his new covenant sacrifice will face a fearful expectation of judgment (10:27, 29–30; 12:25). Ultimately, they were not members of the new covenant people at all.

The new covenant encounter with God at Mount Zion

A significant instance of the term 'covenant' appears in the rhetorical climax of Hebrews (12:18–24), where the author develops an

---

23. On the disputed question as to what is the nature of 'the more severe punishment', see O'Brien, *Hebrews*, p. 380, notes 199–200, and further references.

extended contrast between Israel assembled at Mount Sinai to meet
God (vv. 18–21) and the new covenant encounter with him that
occurs at Mount Zion (vv. 22–24): 'you have come . . . to Jesus, the
mediator of a new covenant' (10:22, 24). In this ultimate eschatological encounter (cf. Rev. 4, 5), God the Judge of all and Jesus, the
mediator of the new covenant, are at the centre of a vast assembly,
comprising myriads of angels and believers of all ages, i.e., those
perfected by the work of Christ, in other words, the 'whole company
of heaven'. Clearly, this 'gathering' is both *heavenly and eschatological.*

Yet Christians in their conversion 'have already come'
(*proserchomai*)[24] to Mount Zion, the city of the Living God, the
heavenly Jerusalem. Our author is telling his listeners that, when
they welcomed the gospel into their lives, they not only came to
God the Judge of all, the joyful assembly of myriads of angels and
the church of the firstborn (10:22–23). They also came to Jesus the
mediator of the new covenant and to his sacrificial death by which
that covenant was sealed (10:24). And, as the mediator who offered
himself in death, Jesus is the reason and basis for their entry into
this joyful heavenly gathering in Mount Zion.

In another sense, however, the heavenly city is still the goal of
the Christian's pilgrimage. The author urges his listeners as pilgrims
to look forward expectantly and so press on to the lasting 'city . . .
that is to come' (13:14; cf. 4:1–11). The letter to the Hebrews reflects
the 'already – not yet' tension found elsewhere in the New Testament,
and this points to the fact that Christians live in the overlap of the
two ages. The mention of 'Jesus the mediator of a new covenant'
appears in a context that is both heavenly and eschatological but
where the 'already' dimension of that tension is strongly accented.

As the listeners and other believers press forward to this joyful
heavenly gathering, they (and we) know that Christ's new covenant
sacrifice has effected a definitive cleansing of our consciences from
the practices and attitudes that belong to the way of death, and

---

24. For an examination of the grammatical, syntactical and contextual
    issues see O'Brien, *Hebrews*, pp. 477–479, 482.

turned aside God's righteous wrath from us. Freed from this awful bondage we are now able to worship and serve the living God – for which we were created – in gratitude to him with reverence and awe (12:28).

2. THE WORD OF GOD

PERFECTLY SPOKEN IN THE SON

Jonathan Griffiths

Hebrews opens with a discussion of how God speaks, and the theme of the word of God is never far in the background throughout the letter.[1] In a brief survey like this, it will not be possible to cover everything that Hebrews says about the character and power of the word of God. What will emerge from this overview of the theme of God's word in Hebrews is a striking line of continuity between God's speech in Scripture, in the person of his Son, and in the writer's own exposition of Scripture. This last point has special significance for preachers whose business it is to expound Scripture week by week.

God's word by the prophets

Hebrews opens with a statement that could be seen as dismissive

---

1. I am very grateful to my grandfather Gerald Griffiths for his kindness in reading and commenting on a draft of this chapter.

of the Old Testament Scriptures: 'Long ago, at many times and in
many ways, God spoke to our fathers by the prophets, but in these
last days he has spoken to us by his Son' (1:1–2). But such an impres-
sion is proved false when we find that the only words of the Son
quoted in Hebrews are in fact Old Testament words, which we are
told the Son 'speaks' now (see, for instance, 2:12–13). Indeed,
Hebrews is full of Old Testament quotations and allusions,
and these are introduced not with the familiar 'it is written' formula,
but with verbs of speaking, generally in the present tense, and
frequently with God the Father, the Holy Spirit, or the Son as the
speaker ('But of the Son he says . . .', 1:8). The writer takes it for
granted that the Old Testament is an 'avowedly incomplete book',[2]
clearly pointing to its own fulfilment in the life and ministry of Jesus.
God continues to speak through those same words that he spoke,
but he speaks them now in the full light of the revealed and
completed work of the Son in these great 'last days' of fulfilment.
God's voice can be heard 'today' (see 4:7) through the words he
spoke in Scripture (see the quotation of Ps. 95 in 4:3, 4:5 and 4:7),
and as we encounter his word, we find that it is 'living and active',
exposing the true state of our heart before God (4:12–13).

God's word by his Son

Following the writer's opening claim that God has 'spoken to us by
[lit. 'in'] his Son' (1:2), we might have expected to see a summary of
the teaching ministry of Jesus or a few key extracts from his most
famous discourses in the Gospels. But instead of giving us a record
of the *words* of Jesus, the rest of the writer's substantial opening
sentence (1:1–4) tells us about the *identity and work* of Jesus: he is the
heir of all things, the agent and sustainer of creation, the perfect
representation of God; he made purification for sins and has taken

---

2. George B. Caird, 'The Exegetical Method of the Epistle to the
   Hebrews', *Canadian Journal of Theology* 5.1 (1959), pp. 44–51, p. 49.

his seat at God's right hand. God's speech through his Son seems to be speech through person and action as much as through spoken word. In fact, Hebrews nowhere (that we can detect) quotes from the incarnate teaching ministry of Jesus. As we have already seen, where we do hear the words of Jesus in Hebrews, they are words he spoke through Old Testament writers.

We are familiar with the idea that Jesus is God's speech in personal form because John's Gospel makes such a claim explicitly: 'In the beginning was the Word, and the Word was with God, and the Word was God' (John 1:1). In his prologue John taps into a stream of biblical material that sees both God's 'word' (*logos* or *rhēma*) and 'wisdom' (*sophia*) as extensions of God's own activity. God's 'word' in the Old Testament creates (Gen. 1; Ps. 33:6), heals (Ps. 107:20) and always accomplishes the purpose God has for it (Isa. 55:11). In the book of Proverbs, God's 'wisdom' too is personified, issuing God's call to the passer-by (Prov. 1:20–33) and working along-side God at creation 'like a master workman' (Prov. 8:22–31). In later Jewish writings, God's wisdom and word are identified with each other,[3] and, more importantly, they move closer towards a fully personalized identity, as we find in the apocryphal work Wisdom of Solomon (Wis. 7:22–30; 18:15–16).

Hebrews never goes as far as John's Gospel does in calling Jesus the 'word', but in the opening verses the writer presents Jesus as being God's word in human form, with his identity and activity giving definitive expression to God's verbally revealed identity and will. More than that, it is interesting to see that in those opening verses Hebrews speaks of Jesus in terms similar to those in which Jewish writers like Philo and the author of Wisdom of Solomon

---

3. See Aristobulus, Fragment 5; Wis. 9:1b–2a; Philo, *Fug.* 97. See also Larry W. Hurtado, *Lord Jesus Christ: Devotion to Jesus in Earliest Christianity* (Cambridge: Eerdmans, 2003), p. 366, esp. n. 31; Andrew Chester, *Messiah and Exaltation: Jewish Messianic and Visionary Traditions and New Testament Christology*, WUNT I.207 (Tübingen: Mohr Siebeck, 2007), p. 50; Harry Austryn Wolfson, *Philo*, 2 vols. (Cambridge, MA: Harvard University Press, 1947), vol. 1, p. 258.

speak of God's 'word' and 'wisdom'. So, for example, Wisdom of Solomon describes 'wisdom' as 'the fashioner of all things' (Wis. 7:22a), while Hebrews says that Jesus is the one 'through whom' God 'created the world' (Heb. 1:2). Wisdom of Solomon describes wisdom as 'a pure emanation of the glory of the Almighty' (Wis. 7:25) and as 'a reflection [*apaugasma*] of eternal light, a spotless mirror of the working of God' (Wis. 7:26), while Hebrews describes Jesus as 'the radiance [*apaugasma*] of the glory of God' (Heb. 1:3).

Similarities in language and imagery between Jewish descriptions of 'word' and 'wisdom' and Hebrews' descriptions of Jesus do add weight to the claim that the writer sees Jesus as giving full expression to God's 'word' and 'wisdom'. However, it is important to note that the writer of Hebrews holds convictions about the identity of Jesus that mean that he and the Jewish writers mentioned ultimately operate in different theological worlds. As F. F. Bruce rightly says, 'while our author's language is that of Philo and the Book of Wisdom, his meaning goes beyond theirs. For them the Logos or Wisdom is the personification of a divine attribute; for him the language is descriptive of a man who had lived and died in Palestine a few decades previously, but who nonetheless was the eternal Son and supreme revelation of God.'[4]

The conviction expressed in 1:1–4 that Jesus is God's word in personal form re-emerges later in Hebrews. In chapters 6 and 7 the writer teaches us that God sometimes speaks to us through promises and oaths, and a careful look at these forms of God's word reveals that Jesus again is at the heart of God's revelation. The writer begins his treatment of promises and oaths in 6:13 by reminding us that, having made a promise[5] to Abraham in Genesis 12:2 and 15:5, God then swore by himself to Abraham in Genesis 22:17, 'I will surely bless you, and I will surely multiply your offspring'. We are then told that 'when God desired to show more convincingly to the heirs of

---

4. F. F. Bruce, *The Epistle to the Hebrews*, NICNT (rev. ed.; Grand Rapids: Eerdmans, 1990), p. 5.

5. The participle *epangeilamenos* is in the aorist.

THE WORD OF GOD 39

the promise the unchangeable character of his purpose, he guaranteed it with an oath' (6:17). The 'heirs' in view here must be Christian believers; the writer has already told his readers that he wants them to imitate those who 'inherit the promises' (6:12). The promise is presumably still the covenant promise to Abraham of Genesis 12:2 and 15:5, and it would make sense to see the oath given for the 'heirs' as being the oath of Jesus' priesthood in the order of Melchizedek from Psalm 110:4 (cited before this passage at Heb. 5:6 and after it at 7:17).

The writer draws particular attention to the fact that God uses both promises and oaths, the oath adding an extra level of confirmation of his intentions (6:13, 17–18).[6] But the nature of the distinction between a divine promise and a divine oath is not immediately clear. To consider the difference, it is helpful to take a closer look at the oath to Abraham of Genesis 22:17, cited in Hebrews 6:14. God gives this oath in the context of restoring Isaac to Abraham after Abraham had shown himself willing to sacrifice him. God tells Abraham not to harm the boy and instead provides a ram for the sacrifice. We read in Genesis 22:14 that 'Abraham called the name of that place, "The Lord will provide"; as it is said to this day, "On the mount of the LORD it shall be provided".' Then follows the divine oath (Gen. 22:15–18). The writer of Hebrews looks back to Abraham's ordeal and the subsequent return of Isaac (on whom the fulfilment of God's earlier promises rested) when he writes that 'Abraham, having patiently waited [or, better, 'endured'], obtained the promise' (Heb. 6:15). In Abraham's case, the difference between God's promise in Genesis 12:2 and 15:5 and God's oath in Genesis 22:15–18 is this: whereas the promise was simply a verbal affirmation of intent, the oath was a verbal affirmation of intent joined with action that brought about its fulfilment. In Genesis 22, God restores Isaac through the provision of an alternative sacrifice at the same time as

---

6. I assume that the 'two unchangeable things' of 6:18 are God's promise to Abraham (to which the Christian addressees are heirs) and his oath of Ps. 110:4 that establishes Jesus' priesthood.

verbally reaffirming his intentions for Abraham in the form of an oath. It was on the occasion of the giving of God's oath that Abraham 'obtained the promise'.

This understanding of an oath seems to stand behind the writer's insistence that God used an oath when he 'desired to *show*' the new covenant heirs of the promise 'the unchangeable character of his purpose' (6:17). When the writer speaks of God's action in taking this oath, he makes use of a rather rare verb,[7] *mesiteuō*, which generally means 'to mediate'. He writes that God 'guaranteed' (or 'mediated', *emesiteusen*) his purpose 'with an oath' (6:17c). The natural rendering of *mesiteuō* is 'to mediate'; the rendering 'to guarantee' lacks clear support in any other ancient literature. However, commentators and translators generally adopt something like 'guarantee' as a more elastic rendering here, presumably because it seems somewhat unnatural to say that God 'mediated his purpose by an oath'.

The more elastic 'guarantee' is not an altogether unhelpful English rendering (for reasons we will see in a moment), but the writer's choice of *mesiteuō* is deliberate and the idea of 'mediation' is central to the notion of the divine oath. If it is correct that the writer's concept of 'oath' (as distinct from promise) involves verbal affirm-ation of intent joined with action, we are prompted to consider here in 6:17 what action is attached to the verbal element of this oath. The use of 'mediation' language in Hebrews helps us a great deal: the term 'mediator' (*mesitēs*) occurs three times in Hebrews (at 8:6, 9:15 and 12:24) and always identifies Jesus, the mediator of the new covenant.[8] A further clue is provided in chapter 7, when the writer returns to explicit treatment of the oath of Psalm 110:4. After quoting part of that oath in 7:21, the writer says that the fact that Jesus was established as priest through that oath 'makes Jesus the

---

7. *Mesiteuō* occurs nowhere else in the NT or LXX.

8. Note the similar movement of thought in 9:15, where Jesus' work as mediator means that 'those who are called may receive the promised eternal inheritance, since a death has occurred . . . ' Here the priestly action of Jesus secures the substance of the promise for the heirs.

guarantor [*engyos*]⁹ of a better covenant' (7:22).¹⁰ God's oath in Psalm 110:4 establishes Jesus as the eternal priest, ensuring the salvation of the heirs of God's promise to Abraham. This oath is no empty word; it issues forth in personal action, that is, the priestly work of Jesus, God's Son.

Just as God's oath to Abraham in Genesis 22 involved his verbal affirmation of intent and his tangible provision of the sacrifice, so too God's oath to the heirs of the promise involves his spoken word and the provision of a priest who would also be the sacrifice. But quite unlike the provision of a ram in Genesis 22, God's action in the oath of Psalm 110:4 is in no sense impersonal or external to himself. In the person of his Son, God himself becomes the mediator between himself and humanity and fully guarantees the salvation of his people by his Son's death in their place and his priestly intercession. Here again we see Jesus as the full and perfect expression of God's spoken word.

Again in chapter 12 the personal nature of God's speech 'by his Son' shines through at the end of the portrait of Zion. The climactic finale of the list of features of this city to which believers have come is 'Jesus, the mediator of a new covenant, and . . . the sprinkled blood that speaks a better word than the blood of Abel' (12:24). The 'speaking' blood of Abel recalls Genesis 4:10 where murdered Abel's shed blood cries out for justice against his guilty brother, Cain.¹¹

---

9. The Greek terms 'guarantor' (*engyos*) and 'mediator' (*mesitēs*) function as virtual synonyms. See C. Spicq, *Notes de Lexicographie Néo-Testamentaire*, Orbis Biblicus et Orientalis 22, 3 vols. (Fribourg: Éditions Universitaires, 1978), vol. 2, pp. 550–551.

10. The rendering of *emesiteusen* in 6:17 as 'guaranteed' is not unhelpful (as I suggested earlier) in the sense that it directs the reader to the conceptual link with 7:22.

11. The final words of Hebrews 12:24 literally read ' . . . sprinkled blood that speaks better than Abel'. Some question whether an allusion to Abel's speaking 'blood' is intended (see discussion of alternatives in P. T. O'Brien, *The Letter to the Hebrews* [Grand Rapids: Eerdmans, 2010], pp. 487–488). However, mention here of speaking blood in conjunction with reference to Abel strongly evokes Gen. 4:10, and I follow the ESV and most other English translations in seeing an ellipsis here and supplying '[blood of] Abel'.

We know already from Hebrews 9 – 10 that the sprinkled blood of Jesus cleanses the worshipper, making him or her acceptable before God. Here in 12:24, the blood of Jesus the 'mediator' speaks a word to God 'the judge of all' (12:23) which is heard by the Christian believer on earth.[12] Whereas Abel's blood cried out to God of Cain's guilt, Jesus' blood cries out to God of the believer's cleansed conscience. Jesus' blood speaks '*in heaven* for us, and from heaven to us'.[13] From the opening of Hebrews we know that the Son's work of making purification for sins (1:3) is central to God's speech through the Son (1:2). We hear God speak and we see his personality and will expressed nowhere more eloquently than in the shed blood of Jesus.

God's word through the writer

Not only does the writer believe that God speaks through Scripture and through the Son; he appears to hold the conviction that God's voice is heard through his own discourse. Strong hints of this conviction emerge at various points in Hebrews. But before we look at the evidence, since this question concerns the character of Hebrews itself, we will first pause and consider what kind of discourse Hebrews actually is.

Hebrews has traditionally been classed as an epistle. It does conclude like a typical New Testament letter, but it lacks the introduction and greetings that usually appear at the opening of a letter, and scholars point to various features of Hebrews that are more characteristic of oral communication than letter-

12. Presumably the message spoken by the blood of Jesus is part and parcel of God's word from heaven that believers must heed for their good and ignore only at their peril (12:25).

13. John Albert Bengel, *Gnomon of the New Testament*, ed. and tr. Andrew R. Fausset, 4 vols. (Edinburgh: T. & T. Clark, [7]1877), vol. 4, pp. 488–489.

writing.[14] The writer designates Hebrews a 'word of exhortation' (*logos tēs paraklēseōs*, 13:22), a term which is used in Acts 13:15 to designate Paul's sermon in the synagogue at Antioch of Pisidia and in a fourth-century liturgy to designate the homily (*Apostolic Constitutions* 8.5; see also 2 Macc. 15:8–11). 'The exhortation' appears as a term on its own in 1 Timothy 4:13 in a context where the congregational gathering is in view and where it probably refers to preaching: 'Until I come, devote yourself to the public reading of Scripture, to exhortation [*tē paraklēsei*], to teaching.' It seems likely that 'word of exhortation' was a recognized term for a sermon in the early church, and we can reasonably surmise that Hebrews was a sermon written from a distance (hence the epistolary elements at the end) and intended to be read out to the congregation. If this is correct, it makes Hebrews especially noteworthy as 'the only example we have in the New Testament of the text of a sermon which has been preserved in its entirety'.[15] In terms of the substance and style of this sermon, there is a case for designating it *an expository sermon*: from beginning to end, it mines texts and themes from the Old Testament for their meaning in light of Christ, applies those texts to the addressees, and exhorts them to respond appropriately.[16]

The writer holds high expectations of what God will accomplish through his sermon. In chapter 3 the writer brings the warning of Psalm 95 to his addressees: 'Therefore, as the Holy Spirit says, "Today,

---

14. Luke Timothy Johnson, *Hebrews: A Commentary*, New Testament Library (Louisville: Westminster John Knox, 2006), p. 10; David E. Aune, *The New Testament in Its Literary Environment* (Cambridge: James Clarke & Co, 1988), p. 213.

15. Albert Vanhoye, *Structure and Message of the Epistle to the Hebrews*, tr. J. Swetnam, Subsidia Biblica 12 (Rome: Editrice Pontificio Instituto Biblico, 1989), p. 3.

16. See R. T. France, 'The Writer of Hebrews as a Biblical Expositor', *TynB* 47.2 (1996), pp. 245–276. Various proposals have been offered to account for the structure of Hebrews and to identify the key Old Testament texts. For an introduction to that discussion, see O'Brien, *Hebrews,* pp. 22–36.

if you hear his voice, do not harden your hearts . . . "' (Heb. 3:7–8).
He then calls upon his hearers to 'exhort one another as long as it is
called "today" . . . ' (3:13) and encourages them to see that at the
present time 'there remains a Sabbath rest for the people of God' (4:9).
In the logic of the quotation from Psalm 95 itself, 'today' is the day
when God's voice is heard. Within the context of the writer's use and
treatment of Psalm 95 in Hebrews, the 'today' of hearing God's voice
would seem to be realized, and the opportunity to respond maintained,
as the writer delivers his sermon. For the wilderness generation (whose
hearing and widespread rejection of God's voice Ps. 95 recalls), God's
word came as a 'message they heard' (4:2). So too for the writer and
the community he addresses: 'For good news came to us just as to
them' (4:3). On the occasion of the delivery of this sermon, God's
voice is surely heard as the sermon is delivered. And knowing that
God's voice is being heard as he preaches,[17] the writer is confident
that the opportunity to respond to God's voice remains; so he exhorts
his addressees, 'Let us therefore strive to enter that rest, so that no one
may fall by the same sort of disobedience' (4:11).

Not only does the writer believe that the delivery of God's word
through his sermon will facilitate the hearing of God's voice, he also
hopes that it will bring about the 'maturity' of his hearers. In 5:11–12
the writer laments the fact that his hearers are not sufficiently mature
in the faith to be able to take on board the more difficult elements
of his teaching. This 'solid food', he explains, 'is for the mature'
(5:14). But, he sets his concerns aside and exhorts his hearers in 6:1,
'let us leave the elementary doctrine of Christ and go on to maturity'.
Significantly for our purposes, 'the writer apparently had some
confidence that God would use his efforts to transform the situation
he addressed'.[18] So, referring back to his hope in 6:1 that his hearers

---

17. Or, at least, as he writes his sermon in the expectation that another
     messenger will read it out.
18. David Peterson, 'God and Scripture', in Paul Helm and Carl Trueman
     (eds.), *The Trustworthiness of God: Perspectives on the Nature of Scripture*
     (Leicester: Apollos, 2002), pp. 118–138, p. 122.

would move on to maturity, and thinking of his teaching in the following chapters, he says, 'this we will do if God permits' (6:3).[19] The author believes that God will use his sermon to bring about his own spiritual maturity and that of his hearers. And as he contemplates his hearers' response to his teaching and their attention to the more difficult material yet to come, he urges on them caution: 'For land that has drunk the rain that often falls on it, and produces a crop useful to those for whose sake it is cultivated, receives a blessing from God. But if it bears thorns and thistles, it is worthless and near to being cursed, and its end is to be burned' (6:7–8). The writer urges his readers to take due care as they listen to his sermon, even to respond to it 'with as much care and diligence as to the Scriptures'.[20]

His concern that his hearers should give due attention to what he says stems from his conviction that God's voice is heard through his sermon. This becomes apparent again at 12:25 where the writer exhorts his hearers, 'See that you do not refuse him who is speaking.' The subject of the participle *ton lalounta* is not identified. Over the course of 12:25–26 it becomes clear that God is the ultimate speaker who must be heeded; the warning spoken of in 12:25b must issue from the one whose voice shook the earth at Sinai and who promises to shake the heavens and the earth at the last day (12:26). But in 12:25a it is not immediately clear who the speaker is: is it God himself, or is it the preacher who addresses his hearers? 'In an ultimate sense, the one who is speaking is God, but those addressed by Hebrews do not hear God speaking in an unmediated way. Therefore, the appeal not to refuse the word of God calls for attention to the human speaker who delivers his word.'[21] The people

---

19. *Poiēsomen* is probably a plural of authorship; but even if it is a standard plural ('we together will do this . . . '), the point is still that the writer expects this movement forward to take place as he expounds God's word.

20. Peterson, 'God and Scripture', p. 122.

21. Craig R. Koester, *Hebrews*, AB 36 (New York: Doubleday, 2001), p. 552; So too Gene R. Smillie, '"The One Who is Speaking" in Hebrews 12:25', *TynB* 55.2 (2004), pp. 275–294, pp. 292–293.

must not refuse God as he speaks to them; but in the moment of hearing the sermon, God's voice is heard as his word is expounded, and thus they must not ignore the preacher as he delivers God's word.

Given what we have seen of the writer's belief that God's voice is heard through his sermon, it is interesting to notice the way in which he identifies his sermon with God's word through the use of the Greek word *logos* ('word', 'message') to identify his sermon. The term *logos* appears in Hebrews at 2:2; 4:2, 12, 13; 5:11, 13; 6:1; 7:28; 12:19; 13:7, 17, 22. In most of these cases, '*logos* refers to a speech or a reality that takes its origin in God' (this is clearly so at 2:2; 4:2, 12; 5:13; 6:1; 7:28; 12:19; 13:7).[22] In these cases, *logos* functions as a theologically significant term (as it does frequently in the New Testament) to identify God's 'word' to us, especially the gospel message. At 13:17 *logos* forms part of a commercial idiom that means 'account to be rendered', and is not relevant to us here. At 5:11 and 13:22 (and quite possibly at 4:13)[23] the term *logos* identifies the writer's own message. Given the considerable consistency with which the writer uses the term *logos* to identify God's word, and given the evidence we have seen above for the writer's view that God's voice is heard through his sermon, it seems significant that he would refer to his sermon using the term *logos*: he believes that as he expounds the Scriptures for his hearers, he is speaking God's 'word' to them.

The ongoing ministry of God's word

The writer describes his own work as that of 'exhortation': he 'exhorts' (*parakalō*) his hearers to bear with his 'word of exhortation'

---

22. O'Brien, *Hebrews*, p. 175.

23. The interpretation of the final clause of 4:13, *pros hon hēmin ho logos*, is much debated. The two main options are that it means 'to whom we must render account' or 'concerning whom is my message' (translations mine). I tend toward the latter as the more natural rendering of the Greek, but both have support among commentators.

(*logos tēs paraklēseōs*) in 13:22. As we have seen, this is a noble and vital
task, in a sense partnering with God in his own 'exhortation' of his
children through his word (see 12:5). The writer insists that this work
of exhortation must continue in the church: 'encourage one another
daily' (3:13, trans. mine); 'let us consider how to stir up one another
to love and good works, not neglecting to meet together, as is the
habit of some, but encouraging one another' (10:24–25). Members
of the church are to encourage 'each other' in the same way that
God encourages his people and as the writer encourages his hearers
– through bringing God's word to them.

But the writer indicates that leaders have a special role to play:
'Obey your leaders and submit to them, for they are keeping watch
over your souls, as those who will have to give an account' (13:17).
The whole section 13:7–19 has as its framework the hearers' attitude
to their leaders (although it goes beyond this theme in vv. 10–16).
By including the request that his hearers should pray for him (v. 18),
the writer places himself alongside the other leaders of the church
to whom he is writing. How has this writer 'kept watch' over the
souls of this congregation? During this time of separation at least
(see 13:19), he has done so through his sermon sent from a distance.
Like leaders of former times 'who spoke to you the word of God'
(13:7), this church leader has faithfully done the same. And so as he
contemplates the 'account' that he will have to give for their souls,
he can say that he has 'a clear conscience' (13:18).[24]

Church leaders who expound God's word and through their
teaching keep watch as shepherds over the souls of his people have
a special mandate from God – they are to be 'obeyed' in so far as
they are serving as faithful spokesmen of God, bringing his word
to his people. Indeed, this should come as no surprise because there
is no room for 'refusing' the God who speaks (12:25ff.). As a

---

24. The writer's claim to have a clear conscience probably has a broader
    reference to his general conduct; but it surely includes in its scope his
    faithful leadership of this congregation through speaking God's word
    to them in his sermon.

preacher, then, the writer carries out a function that continues in the church today, and so his expectation that God's voice is heard and his work is accomplished through the faithful exposition of Scripture is an expectation that present-day preachers may share. That should come as a great encouragement to us who are involved in the work of preaching: it is a tremendous privilege to act as God's spokesmen and to see his word at work changing lives as we preach it faithfully.

However, we must add a note of caution as well. We must also recognize in the Hebrews sermon something that is unique and unrepeatable: not only was this writer a preacher of God's word, he was also an inspired author of Scripture. Whether he recognized it or not, through him God was speaking his very words to be recorded for future generations. We see the clear marks of unique divine inspiration in Hebrews not least through its definitive articulation of key elements of the relationship between old covenant and new. This hermeneutical achievement is not something that can be repeated. In this sense we see in Hebrews the marks of foundational 'prophecy' (cf. Eph. 2:20).[25]

But as a model of Christian preaching, we have a great deal to learn from Hebrews. The writer delighted in 'mining' Scripture for all its meaning and riches. He was convinced that the whole of Scripture concerns the Lord Jesus Christ and the gospel. He was a teacher of doctrine, but never went far between bursts of warning and encouragement; and he clearly loved the people God gave him to shepherd.

© Jonathan Griffiths, 2012

---

25. I am grateful to David Peterson for his helpful comments on some of the issues addressed in this paragraph.

3. THE PRIESTHOOD OF CHRIST

A SERVANT IN THE SANCTUARY

Richard B. Gaffin, Jr

A distinct overtone in Hebrews is now that 'in these last days', God 'has spoken to us in his Son' (1:2), things are 'better' (*kreissōn*). Of the nineteen occurrences of this comparative in the New Testament, thirteen are in Hebrews. The new covenant, vis à vis the old or first, is a 'better covenant' (7:22; 8:6) and so involves a 'better hope' (7:19), 'better promises' (8:6), 'better sacrifices' (9:23, a generic plural for the one sacrifice of Christ), a 'better possession' (10:34), a 'better homeland' (11:16), a 'better resurrection' (11:35). All told, God's consummate self-revelation in his Son has brought about 'something better' (11:40).[1]

This 'betterness' is specified in 10:34 and 11:16 as constituting what is 'abiding' or 'lasting' (*menon*) and 'heavenly'. In terms of the typology the writer introduces in chapters 9 and 10, the new covenant is 'better' because it brings reality and finality, in contrast

---

1. Unless otherwise noted, all translations follow the English Standard Version with occasional minor modifications of my own.

to the old, which is marked by no more than provisional types and passing shadows.[2] From this it can be seen that the use of the comparative 'better' amounts to rhetorical understatement for the unmistakably superlative note the writer sounds at the outset and maintains throughout. God's 'last days' eschatological Son-speech is of an order that is simply incapable of being superseded or transcended. Within this setting of what is 'better' about the new covenant the writer gives a pre-eminent place to Christ's high-priestly work.

Hebrews refers to Christ as both 'priest' (*hiereus*) and 'high priest' (*archiereus*), with the latter being predominant (at just under 70% of the total occurrences of the two words). It might be argued that 'high priest' has in view a comparison, expressed or implied, with Aaron specifically, while 'priest' intends a contrast with the Levitical priesthood as a whole. But 8:3–4 shows that such a distinction does not hold up at every point. Any distinction there may be is not a hard and fast one. For instance, the Levitical priesthood is said to be 'the order of Aaron' (7:11); Aaron is the key figure who represents not just other high priests but the entire priestly order.

Also, while most of the references to Christ as 'priest' occur where the writer applies to him the quotation of Psalm 110:4, 'You are a priest forever after the order of Melchizedek' (5:6; 7:15, 17, 21), this passage is also alluded to where he is referred to specifically as high priest (5:10; 6:20). So, whatever differences in accent there may be between them, the two designations are used interchangeably. Since the writer uses 'high priest' preponderantly, for substantive reasons we will be noting, I will also.

In the overall profile of New Testament teaching only Hebrews calls Christ a (high) priest. However, that this designation does not occur elsewhere hardly means the idea is foreign to the rest of the

---

2. For a penetrating discussion of the writer's typology, see Geerhardus Vos, *The Teaching of the Epistle to the Hebrews* (Grand Rapids: Eerdmans, 1956), pp. 55–65.

New Testament. For the writer, as we will see, the twin related aspects of priestly activity are sacrifice and intercession and these are clearly applied to Christ elsewhere in the New Testament. To do little more here than note relevant passages, see Matthew 20:28 and Mark 10:45; Matthew 26:28 with parallels in Mark and Luke; John 1:29; 10:11, 15; Ephesians 5:2, 25; 1 Timothy 2:5–6; Titus 2:14; 1 John 1:7; Revelation 1:5. These passages, some more clearly than others, all point to the sin-bearing and expiating character of Christ's sacrifice of himself. The key notion of Christ as mediator reinforces this link. In Paul Christ as the 'mediator between God and men' gave himself 'as a ransom for all' (1 Tim. 2:5–6), while for Hebrews Christ's functioning as a high priest, including his self-sacrifice, figures prominently in his being the mediator of the new covenant (8:6; 9:15; 12:24).

Christ's intercession is likewise present elsewhere in the New Testament, both in the past during his early ministry (Luke 22:31–32; John 17) and presently as ascended (Rom. 8:34; 1 John 2:1). The descriptions of the church as a 'holy priesthood' for the purpose of offering 'spiritual sacrifice' and as a 'royal priesthood (1 Pet. 2:5, 9; cf. Rev 1:6; 20:6) presuppose and have the priesthood of Christ for their foundation.

This brief survey shows that the idea of Christ as a priest, as fulfilling priestly functions, is hardly foreign or lacking in the rest of the New Testament. Still, unique to Hebrews is not only its explicit use of the terminology of priesthood but also the centrality of the idea to the writer's Christology, expressed in his presentation both of Christ's person and his work. In this regard the writer provides 'a certain plus in the apprehension of Jesus' saving significance'.[3] Highlighting something of this 'plus' is our interest in this chapter.

---

3. Geerhardus Vos, *Redemptive History and Biblical Interpretation. The Shorter Writings of Geerhardus Vos*, ed. Richard B. Gaffin, Jr (Phillipsburg: P. & R. Publishing, 1980), p. 205.

Christ as high priest in heaven

The timing of his high priesthood

When, according to Hebrews, does the (high) priesthood of Christ begin? This may seem a somewhat odd question given the last of the preceding points. Addressing it, however, is worthwhile not only because some have occasionally taken the view that the writer does not see Christ's priestly work beginning until his ascension. But also, and more importantly, doing so brings to light a key emphasis of the writer.

From time to time some have denied that Hebrews teaches that Christ's death is sacerdotal. For instance, going back to the time of the Reformation and since, some in the Socinian tradition and others that share its rejection of Christ's death as an atonement by penal substitution, have maintained that the writer detaches Christ's sacrificial death from his priestly activity, which in their view only begins subsequently with his ascension and consists in exercising a generally favourable influence on God.

Suffice it here to say that this view, particularly its vacating Christ's sacrificial death of any sacerdotal significance, is hardly sustainable in the light of passages like 9:11–12, 24–26; 10:10–12; 13:12. While it may be true that none of them *explicitly* calls Christ a priest or otherwise designates his death as priestly, there can be little question that within their immediate contexts and the letter as a whole, his self-sacrifice is essential to his high priestly activity. How, concretely, the writer conceives of that organic connection will be noted presently. We may fairly conclude, then, that in Hebrews Christ's death is priestly in nature. His sacrificial death is integral to his identity and activity as high priest, a *sine qua non*. Without it the latter would not and could not exist.

Still, with that observed and kept clear, the writer places great weight on the phase of Christ's priestly work that begins with the ascension, on Christ as presently a high priest *in heaven*. This emphasis, it is worth noting, contrasts with the often prevailing accent in the history of the church, especially in the modern era to the present, focused (necessarily) on maintaining and defending Christ's death as a sacerdotal sacrifice of substitution that atones for sin.[4]

In fact, his emphasis is such that the writer even makes statements that by themselves could be taken to suggest that Christ was not a high priest until after his death. For instance: 'Therefore he had to be made like his brothers in every respect, so that he might become a merciful and faithful high priest in the service of God, to make propitiation for the sins of the people' (2:17). Here, we are told, it was incumbent on Christ to become like his brothers 'in all respects' (*kata panta*). Within the immediate context, particularly verse 14, this comprehensive likeness includes experiencing death. This sweeping conformity (sin excepted, 4:15), then, is to the end that as a *consequence* he might thereby '*become*' (*genētai*) a high priest, merciful and faithful in what he is doing presently, continuously, particularly in now being able, as himself having been fully exposed to temptation (4:15), to aid those being tempted (2:18). In other words, his life of suffering, including his death, are prerequisites for his priesthood which is seen to consist in functions that he begins discharging only after being made like his brothers 'in every respect'.

What about the reference to propitiation in 2:17 on this reading? First, it should not be missed that the writer shares the understanding of other New Testament writers that Christ's death is propitiatory (e.g., Rom. 3:25; 1 John 2:2), that is, effective in removing the God's just and holy wrath on sinners. Further, however, it appears that '*hilaskesthai* does not here denote the single act of atonement on the cross, but the subsequent activity whereby the Savior continually applies the propitiatory power of His sacrifice'. 'The reference is not to the sacrifice of Calvary, but to the

---

4. Certainly both aspects – the earthly and the heavenly, sacrifice and intercession – have been recognized. In the confessional legacy of the church, balanced statements can be found, e.g., *Westminster Larger Catechism*, Q.44, *Shorter Catechism*, Q.25.

intercessory work of Christ as priest which is now being exercised in heaven.'[5]

Commentators, characteristically, do not follow Vos on this point and instead see a reference to Christ's propitiatory death. However, I find his proposal plausible, even persuasive, in view of the immediate context (2:14–16), where, as we have noted following Vos, his death is included in being 'made like his brothers in every respect' as the prerequisite for his being 'a merciful and faithful high priest'. To be taken into account as well is the progressive or continuous aspect of the present tense infinitive the writer uses. This understanding in no way takes away from the propitiatory efficacy and finality of Christ's once-for-all sacrificial death, about which, as we have already noted, the writer elsewhere is not only clear but emphatic (e.g., 7:27; 9:26, 28; 10:12, 14).

'And being made perfect, he became the source of eternal salvation to all who obey him, being designated by God a high priest after the order of Melchizedek' (5:9–10). Here Christ's being 'designated' as high priest is correlative with his having become the 'source of eternal salvation', as both, in turn, are the consequence of his obedience in the face of suffering that culminated in his death (5:7–8). Being designated high priest, then, is seen as taking place subsequent to his death, in his exaltation. In the immediate context verse 5 confirms this: 'Christ did not *exalt* himself to be made a high priest', but was 'appointed' such in the resurrection (Ps. 2:7 is best understood as being taken by the writer to apply to the 'begetting' into the new and final phase of sonship that took place in Christ's resurrection; cf. 1:5).

In 6:19–20 readers are encouraged with ' . . . a hope that enters into the inner place behind the curtain, where Jesus has gone as a forerunner on our behalf, having become a high priest forever after the order of Melchizedek'. Here Jesus' *becoming* a high priest is associated with his entrance into the heavenly sanctuary. This entry, the writer subsequently makes clear, especially in chapters 9 and 10, took

---

5. Vos, *Redemptive History*, p. 145; Vos, *Teaching*, p. 102.

place at the time of his ascension. In the same vein is the categorical counterfactual in 8:4, 'Now if he were on earth, he would not be a priest at all . . . '

So, when for the writer does Christ become a high priest? On balance, the overall answer lies in appreciating what has been aptly dubbed the 'ritual geography'[6] that structures his thinking. The argumentation developed particularly in 9:1 – 10:18 shows that the annual Day of Atonement ritual in Israel under the old covenant (Lev. 16) prefigures and provides the model or pattern that shapes the writer's understanding of Christ's work as high priest. According to this ritual in its basic outline, recounted by the writer in 9:1–10, blood from the animals sacrificed outside the Most Holy Place of the tabernacle atoned only by then being taken inside, beyond the dividing curtain, and sprinkled there on and around the mercy seat by the high priest.

Christ certainly differs markedly from these old covenant high priests. Among other respects, his once-for-all sacrifice for sin is the final and consummate reality to which the annual repetition of the shadowy Day of Atonement ritual could do no more than point. Further, unlike those high priests, his sacrifice consists in offering himself. Still, the atoning efficacy of his high priestly self-sacrifice is according to the pattern set by them. That efficacy resides not only in his death on earth, outside the true, heavenly tabernacle, but also in his appearing and presenting himself as sacrificed in heaven, in the inner sanctum of that tabernacle, at the right hand of God (9:23–24). His sacrifice on earth, absolutely necessary, has no need of being repeated, but its efficacy depends on his perpetual presence in heaven.

In Hebrews, then, Christ is a (high) priest both because of what he did in the past, on earth and also because of what he is doing now, in heaven. But the stress is on the latter, on the present activity of Christ as high priest in the heavenly sanctuary. In fact, risking misunderstanding, we may say that for the writer Christ is a high priest

---

6. Vos, *Teaching*, p. 113.

not so much because of what he did on earth in the past but especially
because of what he is doing in heaven now. His accent is such that
Christ's priestly death, unquestionably and essentially necessary, is by
itself in a way preliminary and preparatory to the distinct, new and
climatic stage of priesthood that begins with his exaltation, so much
so that it is as if he were not a high priest until then.

In the course of his lengthy treatment of Christ's work in his
Reformed Dogmatics Herman Bavinck observes, 'In the state of exaltation there still remains much for Christ to do.'[7] This striking
statement, surely faithful to Scripture as a whole, is especially true
to the emphasis of Hebrews. Yet we may ask whether, with its
implications, it has been developed and functioned in the theology,
preaching and life of the church as it should. The 'it is finished' of
the cross (John 19:30) is true, crucially true. It points to the end
of his humiliation and, together with his resurrection, to remission
of sin and entitlement to eschatological life as definitively achieved
and secured. But it is only *relatively* true, relative to the 'much', as
Bavinck says, which it remains for the exalted Christ to do. That
'much' extensively occupies the writer of Hebrews.

The centrality of his high priesthood

The pivotal role of Christ as the heavenly high priest is clear from
8:1–2:

> Now the main point in what we are saying is this: we have such a high
> priest, one who is seated at the right hand of the throne of the Majesty
> in heaven, a servant in the sanctuary, in the true tent that the Lord set up,
> not man.

Christ as high priest in heaven, the writer says, is his 'main point'
(as *kephalaion* is best translated here) 'in the things being said' (*tois
legomenois*), or as we may fairly paraphrase in light of the present

7. Herman Bavinck, *Reformed Dogmatics*, ed. John Bolt, tr. John Vriend, 4
    vols. (Grand Rapids: Baker Academic, 2006), vol. 3, p. 568, cf. p. 570.

participle, 'in what we are in the midst of saying'. The range of this prepositional phrase, how broad a sweep it has, is not made explicit here and is best gauged by assessing the flow of the discourse in Hebrews as a whole. With little, if any, question, the phrase plausibly refers to the large central section, 4:14 – 10:31. But considering that Christ as high priest comes into view on either side of this section, at 2:17 – 3:1 (in fact pointing back all the way to 1:3) on the one side and at 13:11ff. on the other, it will not be too far off the mark to apply 8:1–2 to the entire book. In the writer's own view, then, Christ's heavenly high priestly ministry is, as much as any, the main point of Hebrews as a whole.

Joining another overall observation to this conclusion sheds an important light on the central role the writer gives to Christ's high priesthood. The genre of Hebrews has a somewhat mixed character, which has prompted various views. Is it a letter or a sermon? It begins like the latter but ends like the former. But however we further assess this epistolary-homiletic format, the writer provides us with his own description of the document. Drawing towards a close, he says in 13:22, 'I urge you, brothers, bear with the word of exhortation, for I have written to you briefly.' As more careful exegesis will show, here 'the word of exhortation' is best taken to refer to the document as a whole. All told, then, according to the writer himself Hebrews is basically hortatory, essentially parenetic.

It is easy to see just how appropriate this designation is. Not only are imperatives pervasive throughout but they are in a way that structure the discourse as a whole. That shaping factor can be seen, for instance, by reading together the following string of fundamental or 'first order' exhortations: 2:1, 3; 3:1, 12–14; 4:1, 14, 16; 6:1, 11–12; 10:26–29, 35–36; 12:1, 5–6, 15, 25.

Undeniably Hebrews contains considerable and profound teaching concerning Christ's person and work, especially his high priestly identity and activity. As the author wrote 'he had in mind a well defined doctrinal system'.[8] But Hebrews is not aptly viewed, as

---

8. Vos, *Teaching*, p. 69.

it has often been traditionally, as a doctrinal treatise, primarily about the priesthood of Christ and the superiority of the new covenant to the old. Rather, as it has been neatly put, in Hebrews 'thesis serves parenesis'; ' . . . parenesis takes precedence over thesis in expressing the writer's purpose'.[9] In Hebrews, we may say, doctrine is always present 'in solution' with application.

This brings us to the following important overarching conclusion: 8:1–2 and 13:22 form the axes around which the study of Hebrews as whole ought to revolve. These verses define the matrix within which the writer develops his teaching; they set the parameters that fix the area of his overall concern. For any study of Hebrews, then, not only when our interest is in Christ as high priest, a helpful point of departure is to view it as a 'word of exhortation' in which the heavenly high priestly ministry of Christ is 'the main point'.

A further question

This conclusion prompts the following question: if Christ is the exalted high priest, with all that entails in terms of his present redemptive triumph and his accomplishment of a salvation that is settled and secure, why is the hortatory element so prominent, why the need for the imperatives that permeate the document? Or, put more simply, if the present heavenly high priestly ministry is its 'main point', why is the book as a whole a 'word of exhortation'?

The answer lies in recognizing that in Hebrews the imperatives are, so to speak, indicative of an indicative. The pervasive exhortations, especially those with a more fundamental sweep, point to a state of affairs, to a basic aspect of the present circumstances of the church. The writer, in other words, contemplates Christ's high priestly ministry not in the abstract but in light of the present

---

9. William L. Lane, *Hebrews*, WBC 47, 2 vols. (Dallas: Word, 1991) vol. 1, p. c; cf. Vos, *Teaching*, p. 69: 'It [the document] expresses a firm belief in the efficacy of *doctrine* as a means of grace . . . In Hebrews doctrine is never introduced for its own sake . . . ' (emphasis original).

situation of the church, a situation for which he deems such exhortation not only relevant but necessary.

What is that situation as the writer sees it? The answer in large part is provided in the section 3:7 – 4:13, where, in an interpretive handling of Psalm 95:7–11 with the inclusion of Genesis 2:2, he makes a large-scale redemptive-historical comparison between old covenant Israel and the new covenant church. He does that by drawing the analogy at a specific point in Israel's history, to the experience of the wilderness generation.[10] This comparison has two sides to it. On the one hand, the church has had a real experience of salvation (cf. 2:3, 10; 5:9; 6:9). It has already been set free from the bondage of sin, from its guilt and dominating power, pictured by Israel's exodus from slavery in Egypt. The 'last days', eschatological deliverance from sin promised in the gospel, is a present reality for the church.

At the same time, however, just as Israel in the wilderness, freed from slavery, had not yet entered into the Promised Land (the 'rest' of Canaan; see, e.g., Deut. 12:9–10; Josh. 1:13–15), so the church does not yet enjoy God's 'rest' (4:9). It has not received eschatological salvation in its full and final form.[11] The church's present possession of salvation is certain and secure, but it is not yet unthreatened and unchallenged. For now, between Christ's ascension and return (e.g., 9:26, 28), as the people of God they are a wilderness congregation, a pilgrim people. In the duress of their present desert circumstances hardships and trials are pervasive. These stressful testings are carried with them and conspire together toward the

---

10. For some expansion of these comments on the writer's use of this analogy, see my 'A Sabbath Rest Still Awaits the People of God', in Charles Dennison and Richard Gamble (eds.), *Pressing Toward the Mark: Essays Commemorating Fifty Years of the Orthodox Presbyterian Church* (Philadelphia: The Committee for the Historian of the Orthodox Presbyterian Church, 1986), pp. 33–51, esp. pp. 34–47.

11. *In this passage* references to 'rest' are entirely future for the church in its present wilderness existence; see Gaffin, 'Sabbath Rest', pp. 38–39, 44–46.

ultimate temptation, as Israel faced in the wilderness, to abandon
their faith and rebel against God in unbelief (e.g., 3:12–13). So, there
is every need to 'hold fast', to persevere (e.g., 3:6, 8, 14; 4:1, 11, 14;
10:23, 36).

This necessity finds particularly striking expression in 3:14: 'For
we share in Christ, if indeed we hold our original confidence firm
to the end.' The perfect indicative of the main clause or consequent
('we have become partakers of Christ') is linked with a future conditional clause ('if we hold fast . . . to the end'; cf. 3:6c). Here the
perfect (past) indicative of salvation, belonging to Christ, is made
contingent on the future condition of perseverance. The syntax
reflects what can be characterized as the conditioned certainty, the
'contingent confidence' (Dennis Johnson),[12] taught throughout
Hebrews.

It is this present wilderness identity and situation of the New
Testament church, with the attendant need to persevere in faith, that
provides the rationale, indeed the necessity, for the writer's repeated
exhortations. That, in turn, provides in large measure the rationale,
indeed the absolute necessity, for Christ's high priestly work as the
writer considers it, the reason he stresses its present heavenly aspect.

The question, as pressing as it is practical, is where those who are
'partakers of Christ' are to find the resources for holding fast, for
persevering in faith. With that urgent concern the writer ultimately
directs his readers, notably, not to their faith, nor to resources
resident in the Christian community, nor to their persevering efforts
of whatever sort, praying or otherwise, as important as all these are,
but to his 'main point'. He would have them understand that they
must stay focused and dependent on the resources, more than
adequate, of the high priest they have in heaven, on Christ, who
'after he has appeared once for all at the end of the ages to put away
sin by the sacrifice of himself' 'has entered . . . into heaven itself,
now to appear in the presence of God for us' (9:26, 24).

---

12. In unpublished notes of class lectures at Westminster Seminary
California, 1987.

This appearance in heaven involves two decisive aspects: first, his permanent presence or presentation of himself alive in the heavenly sanctuary, at the right hand of God, in the efficacy of his finished, once-for-all self-sacrifice for sin, and second his perpetual intercession or intercessory presence there based on that self-sacrifice. In the heavenly sanctuary Christ is 'able to save to the uttermost those who draw near to God through him, since he always lives to make intercession for them' (7:25). Because this sanctuary service is unfailing in its efficacy, they hold fast to the end, they do persevere in faith, they will not cease being partakers of Christ.

Son and high priest

Any treatment of Christ's priesthood in Hebrews needs to keep in view the link with his sonship. For while high priest is the dominant or central Christological conception, Son of God is more basic. Unless that is appreciated, the result will be an inadequate understanding of the exalted nature and uniqueness of his high priestly ministry. We are alerted to this link implicitly already in the writer's opening words in 1:1–2a, an overarching umbrella statement that covers everything said in the document as a whole. Christ's work as high priest has the prominence the writer subsequently gives it because of its central place in God's consummate 'last-days' revelation 'in the Son'.

The rest of 1:2 and the beginning of verse 3 go on to describe the Son in his full eternal and essential deity and as the creator and sustainer of the universe – in as emphatic and explicit language as anywhere in Scripture. But the end of verse 3 also has in view implicitly his fully assumed humanity (cf. 2:14, 17; 4:15). As the Son he had 'made purification for sins'. Further, verse 4 immediately adds, a decisive consequence of this priestly sacrifice of the Son is that in his ascension he has become superior to the angels on the order of his having 'inherited a more excellent name than theirs'. In light of the use of Psalm 2:7 (together with 2 Sam. 7:14) in verse 5, this inherited name is best understood as 'son'. The exaltation of the Son as priest involves a 'begetting' in the sense that it ushers him into a new and final phase of sonship. Because the Son is now 'at the right hand of the Majesty on high', his priestly ministry takes on an efficacy that is unprecedented and unsurpassable.

This climactic tie is highlighted subsequently in 3:1–6. Within the setting of God's single covenant-historical house-building project with its basic twofold old and new covenant, anticipatory and final divisions, readers are to consider Jesus as the high priest of their confession (v. 1). They are to do that as, in contrast to Moses' fidelity within that house, 'Christ is faithful as Son over his house' (vv. 5–6). In 4:14 they are to hold fast their confession since their 'great high priest' who has ascended is 'Jesus the Son of God'.

No doubt the most arresting instance of the link between Christ as Son and high priest involves the writer's references to Melchizedek. That Christ is 'a priest forever, after the order of Melchizedek' is introduced for the first time in 5:6 as a direct quote of Psalm 110:4, cited there to highlight the significance of his exaltation for his priesthood, with the same thought expressed in 5:10 and then again in 6:20.

The latter reference provides a transition that serves to trigger much of what is said in chapter 7. Verses 1–10 develop the reference to Melchizedek, the significance of his person and activity, while verses 11–28 provide the first extended statement of the superiority or perfection of the priesthood of Christ to the Levitical priesthood, as the former is 'according to the order of Melchizedek', the latter 'according to the order of Aaron' (v. 11).

Set in this context 7:1–3 reads:

> For this Melchizedek, king of Salem, priest of the Most High God, met
> Abraham returning from the slaughter of the kings and blessed him,
> and to him Abraham apportioned a tenth part of everything. He is first,
> by translation of his name, king of righteousness, and then he is also
> king of Salem, that is, king of peace. He is without father or mother or

> genealogy, having neither beginning of days nor end of life, but
> resembling the Son of God he continues a priest forever.

In the Greek text, masked in English translations, this is a single
long sentence, 'For this Melchizedek ... remains a priest forever',
with everything in between a series of single predicates and predicate
clauses that modify the subject 'Melchizedek'.

This sentence raises interesting and difficult questions and has
provoked considerable discussion. For preaching and teaching it is
important not to become so preoccupied with the details of this
discussion as to miss that the writer's references to Melchizedek all
function to make a single profound yet simply stated point: to say
that Christ is a priest according to the order of Melchizedek is to
say that as a priest he is in a class by himself. His priesthood is unique.
No one else is or can be a high priest according to the order of
Melchizedek.

These verses are the writer's reflection on the incident of the
priest-king blessing Abram, recorded in Genesis 14:17–20, made in
the light of Psalm 110:4. A guideline for interpreting them is to
recognize that he is not involved in esoteric speculation. In that
regard the series of predicates in 7:3 has given rise to the greatest
speculation. Beginning in the early church, a manifestation of the
Holy Spirit, of the Father, of the pre-incarnate Christ, an angel in
human form, another kind of intermediate being, have all been
proposed for the figure of Melchizedek. But he is not a mysterious
being, 'a biological anomaly' (F. F. Bruce). Rather, he is a true, no
more than human, contemporary of Abram.

The writer is interested in the historical person Melchizedek
because of the significance he has as a type in his capacity as a priest-
king, a significance with which the writer sees him invested in
Psalm 110:4, and by which he points to Christ. In other words, the
predicates in 7:3 apply to his person in terms of his official significance. As an office bearer (priest-king) he is without parents or
genealogy, etc. The typological point that bears on Christ and his
priesthood is found at the point of contrast with the Levitical

priesthood where genealogy and proper parentage, being a priest for a limited time in a line of succession established and regulated by the Mosaic law, is essential and determinative (cf. Lev. 21:13–14; Neh. 7:64). Verse 6 confirms that family pedigree and ordered succession is the central point of the contrast. 'The one who is not descended from them' sums up matters (cf. 'without genealogy' [*agenealogētos*], 7:3).

In his role as a type Melchizedek is 'made like (*aphōmoiōmenos*) the Son of God' (v. 3). The verbal force of the perfect passive participle ('made like'), veiled in the ESV ('resembling') and NIV ('like'), should be maintained. A key for understanding is to recognize that here 'the Son of God' is *not* a reference to the incarnate Christ, to Christ in his appearance in history. The writer is quite clear: the historical Christ is 'according to the order of Melchizedek'; Christ incarnate is 'made like' Melchizedek, not the reverse. Rather, here 'the Son of God' designates his eternal and divine existence (cf. 1:2b–3, 6–12).

The writer's point, then, is that the historical person Melchizedek, 'made like the Son of God', is a type of the eternal Son. He functions typologically in two respects. First, in his greatness, seen in the fact that Abraham gave him tithes (7:4; he received tithes from Abraham, 7:6). This was an act of religious homage by the father of all believers (cf. 'the seed of Abraham', 2:16) and through him indirectly by the Levitical priesthood (7:5, 9–10) that acknowledged the greater religious dignity of the 'priest of the Most High God', Melchizedek. This greatness is also seen in his blessing Abraham (7:7).

The typical function of Melchizedek also appears in the aura of eternity surrounding his person in Genesis 14, that is, by what the Genesis narrative does *not* say, giving rise to a kind of negative theology for the writer in the string of negative predicates in verse 3. Here it is important to keep clear that the Son of God as *person*, in distinction from his office and appearance in history, provides the pattern according to which Melchizedek is made priest-king. An underlying principle of the typology is that dignity of office is based on or follows from worth of person.

The central thread of the writer's argument is that the greatness and eternity of the person of the Son of God determines the typical greatness and eternity appearance of the historical figure Melchizedek and so the character of his priesthood. Further, the priesthood of Christ, historically speaking (in terms of the history of redemption and his actual exercise of priesthood in the past on earth and presently in heaven) is copied according to the order of Melchizedek. Therefore, ultimately, through Melchizedek as the typical link, it is Christ's divine, eternal nature as the Son of God that shapes his priesthood and gives it its uniqueness. His divine, eternal Sonship makes his priesthood what it is in distinction from every other kind of priesthood.

What prompted the writer to introduce the figure of Melchizedek into his argumentation as he does? An answer, if not certain, plausibly begins with recalling that Psalm 110, applied consistently to Christ, is the psalm most frequently cited in the New Testament, whether by direct quotation or allusion. Apparently, then, it functioned with some prominence in the life of the early church at the time Hebrews was written, and so for the first readers a messianic appeal to it would likely have been familiar or even expected. About half of these New Testament citations are in Hebrews (twelve), six of them to verse 1 (the reference to sitting at the Lord's right hand) and six to verse 4 (referring to the priestly order of Melchizedek). Notably, only Hebrews quotes verse 4 (except for a possible allusion in John 12:34); all citations elsewhere (the Gospels, Acts, Paul) are to verse 1.

Given the writer's singular stress on the climatic phase of Christ's high priestly ministry beginning with the ascension, and given that he alone in the New Testament calls Christ a (high) priest, it is hardly surprising (perhaps even inevitable) that he alone in the New Testament connects Psalm 110:1 and 4 or that he reads the Genesis 14 narrative as he does in light of that connection. The interchange of Jesus with the Pharisees in Matthew 22:41–46 is especially instructive at this point. The latter are silenced by his appeal to Psalm 110:1 and the rhetorical question he bases on it ('If then

David calls him Lord, how is he his son?'), a question that contains an implicit claim to deity.

In a similar manner, the writer of Hebrews is concerned to show his readers that while Christ's priesthood according to the order of Melchizedek specifies categorically its uniqueness in distinction to the Levitical priesthood and also entails exaltation to God's right hand, that messianic exaltation is not adequately grasped solely in terms of his humanity; it also and more ultimately entails his deity. Christ is and can be high priest 'according to the order of Melchizedek' only as Melchizedek is 'made like the Son of God'. While the writer's Melchizedek typology may not have been necessary to establish this dimension of deity, it certainly serves to highlight that dimension in a striking fashion.

The writer's final affirmation of the link between Christ's sonship and high priesthood in 7:28 closes the initial elaboration of his 'main point' (8:1): 'For the law appoints men in their weakness as high priests, but the word of the oath, which came after the law, appoints a Son who has been made perfect forever.' In the parallelism of this culminating statement, the superiority of Christ's priesthood, contrasted with the Levitical order, resides in the fact that as a high priest he is the 'Son made perfect forever'. The breadth of the conception of sonship in view here should not be missed. An ontological aspect is intimated: he is Son in contrast to 'men'. There is as well a messianic or functional aspect: given his fully assumed humanity as Son he is 'made perfect' (cf. 2:14–15). As Son and high priest he is true God and true man.

If we ask how more specifically Christ's deity, his eternal sonship, qualifies his high priesthood, from the immediate context (7:26–27) it is that he is properly (*eprepen*) 'holy, innocent, undefiled, separated from sinners' and in his self-sacrifice did not need to offer sacrifices 'first for his own sins' (cf. 'without sin', 4:15). From the wider context, as he is ultimately the eternal Son, an overall design and outcome of his priesthood consists 'in bringing many sons to glory' (2:10). God is eternally determined that the Son have those to share in his glory whom 'he is not ashamed to call . . . brothers' (2:11b).

Or in the closely related teaching of Paul, his predestinating purpose is that there be those 'conformed to the image of the Son, in order that he might be firstborn among many brothers' (Rom. 8:29). To that great end, the Son as high priest is the one who sanctifies them (2:11a) by his propitiatory self-sacrifice and continuing intercessory presence in the heavenly sanctuary.

The perfecting of the Son as high priest highlighted in 7:26 is also present in 2:10 and 5:9. Here we are unable to give this striking notion the attention it deserves but will have to let several brief comments suffice.[13] A key statement for understanding what this perfecting involves is 5:8–10: Jesus' being perfected as high priest is the outcome of a process through which though he was a Son, 'he learned obedience through the things he suffered'.

Several things are plain about this learning process. It was experienced by the Son in his fully assumed humanity ('in the days of his flesh', 5:7). It is quite gratuitous to assume that the writer considered this perfecting pedagogy to have involved needing to unlearn or to learn what was new in principle. Also, while it is ethical in character it is not a matter of general moral development. Specifically, it involved obedience learned in the face of suffering and ever deepened by experience in response to the continuing call of suffering. Nor was such perfecting obedience for his own self-improvement but rather that he might become 'the source (*aitios*) of eternal salvation to all who obey him'. His high priestly obedience as Son is calculated to elicit their obedience as sons.

This passage links closely with 2:17–18, 'since he was tempted [as 'a merciful and faithful high priest'] in what he suffered, he is able to help those who are being tempted' (as this verse ought to be translated; so NASB, NRSV, *contra* ESV, NIV, RSV). As suffering was a school in which he learned the strength of temptation inherent in suffering, so suffering was as well a school in which he learned the strength of obedience that overcomes the temptation proceeding from suffering (Vos). The great high priest-Son has been perfected

---

13. For an extended treatment, see esp. Vos, *Redemptive History*, pp. 143–150.

through his temptation-sufferings. For him they were 'without sin' as their outcome. So he is able to serve with efficacious empathy (4:15) those who are sons in their temptation-sufferings.

Conclusion

'Jesus Christ – the same yesterday, today and forever' (13:8). This climactic affirmation provides a fitting conclusion to any consideration of the priesthood of Christ in Hebrews. Despite the way it is often read, it is not, at least in the first place, a proof text for his divine immutability, that as God he is unchanging, though that attribute is surely in the background (see, for instance, 1:10–12).[14] Rather, it is almost certainly a declaration of his unwavering fidelity and unfailing reliability, and so of the unshakable security he provides for those he serves as high priest – in his once-for-all sacrifice in the past on earth and in his ongoing present and future sanctuary presence and intercession in heaven.

© Richard B. Gaffin, Jr, 2012

---

14. '[N]ot . . . the eternal existence of Christ' (John Calvin, *Commentaries of the Epistle of Paul the Apostle to the Hebrews*, tr. J. Owen [Grand Rapids: Eerdmans, 1948], p. 345); 'not . . . an acclamation of Jesus' timeless ontological immutability' (Lane, *Hebrews*, vol. 2, p. 528).

4. THE TABERNACLE

NO MUSEUM PIECE

David Gooding

Introduction

Why the tabernacle?

It is a striking feature of Hebrews that it makes no mention of the temple at Jerusalem. The words *hieron* and *naos* do not occur in the epistle. Instead it concentrates on the tabernacle which Moses built in the desert.

From this some scholars have deduced that the epistle was not written in the first place to Christian Jews in Jerusalem who still might have been inclined to adhere to the forms of worship in the temple. Instead, the epistle was written to Christian Jews (and perhaps Gentiles) living in, say, Italy, in Rome or elsewhere. Even so, some of these Jews may well have been like the thousands of Christian Jews in Jerusalem who were still 'zealous for the law' (Acts 21:20, ESV).[1]

---

1. Throughout this chapter, English Bible quotations are the author's own translation, unless noted otherwise.

They might even have been in the habit of attending the feasts of the Lord in the temple at Jerusalem – at least once in a lifetime – as did thousands of diaspora Jews (Acts 20:16).

Be that as it may, the prime reason for Hebrews' emphasis on the tabernacle was the historical fact that Israel's traditional form of national worship and of the individual's approach to God went back to the establishment of the old covenant. The tabernacle was designed by God at that time as the fit expression of the worship of people living under the old covenant. It therefore carried the authority of that covenant.

Jews who had recently come to believe that Jesus is the Messiah, and perhaps even met on the first day of the week to commemorate the institution of the new covenant at the Lord's Supper, may not, however, have immediately recognized that the new covenant radically changed their traditional form of worship and approach to God. And when they began to discover the difference, they still might have been afraid to abandon the old, and embrace the new, particularly if the new was frowned on by the majority of the local diaspora Jews (cf. what happened in the synagogue at Pisidian Antioch, Acts 13:44–50).

Hebrews, therefore, will emphasize the radical difference that the new covenant makes in a believer's approach to God; so radical, that a believing Jew will eventually abandon the old system with its earthly tabernacle, Levitical priesthood, animal sacrifices and restricted approach to God, and joyfully accept the new. But Hebrews will do so in an attractive way. It will not denounce Israel's old approach to God as something useless or evil. On the contrary, it will affirm that the Mosaic tabernacle was commanded by God and designed by the Holy Spirit (8:5; 9:8). On the other hand Hebrews will point out that the Mosaic tabernacle had a dual function, what the difference was between the two, and what the relevance of both was to Christians.

The tabernacle's dual function

The tabernacle's first function was to be a copy and shadow of the heavenly things (8:5). This function was like that of a wise, kindly teacher who helps children grasp the abstract truths of mathematics by means of solid, brightly-coloured bricks. Some of the principles thus taught under the tabernacle's first function, moreover, were of permanent validity: such as, for instance, the principle that without shedding of blood there is no forgiveness (9:22). At the same time, the blood of animal sacrifices was only toy-money. It could not actually pay the price of sin.

The second function was to be a shadow of the good things to come (10:1). Simultaneously with the first, this function of the tabernacle, with its priesthood, furniture, rituals and sacrifices, was designed as a system of prophetic symbols or shadows, pointing forward to the coming great reality: the person and work of Christ (10:1). When, therefore, Jesus came, these shadows would help Jews to identify him. They had only to compare the reality with the prophetic shadows and symbols, to be convinced that he was the long-promised Messiah and Saviour. But then the reality would supersede the shadows.

Our aim here

Hebrews 8 – 10 deals at length with a number of profound topics intimately connected with the tabernacle:

1. the superiority of the new covenant over the old covenant, as a result of which the old covenant's tabernacle (9:1) has become obsolete (8:13);
2. the replacement of the Aaronic priesthood by Christ's infinitely superior Melchizedek priesthood (ch. 7; 9:11–14, 25–26);
3. the superiority of the once-for-all sacrifice of Christ's body over the repeated animal sacrifices offered in the tabernacle (9:11–14; 10:1–18).

However, these profound topics are discussed in other chapters in this present volume. In this chapter, therefore, we shall concentrate on the tabernacle building and on its internal arrangements.

But of what practical use for believers today could such a study of the ancient tabernacle building be? After all, Scripture itself admits that the tabernacle and its affairs were at best only 'a shadow of the good things to come' (10:1, ESV). Now that the great reality has come, why should we still concern ourselves with the shadows?

The first answer that Hebrews gives is that the tabernacle was built at God's command as 'a copy and shadow of the heavenly things' (8:5, ESV); therefore a study of it will help us grasp the wonder of a believer's present access into the actual presence of God in heaven, by contrasting it with the very limited access into the Most Holy Place accorded even to the high priests in the pre-Christian tabernacle on this earth. So when Hebrews 8, 9 and 10 reach their climax, the lesson drawn will be: 'Therefore, brothers, since we have confidence to enter the Most Holy Place by the blood of Jesus, by a new and living way opened for us through the curtain, that is, his body . . . let us draw near . . . ' (10:19–22, NIV).

Not all Christians, however, believe that these verses in fact mean that believers have, here and now on earth, spiritual access into the immediate presence of God in heaven. True, Christ himself has bodily entered heaven, but we his people, they hold, cannot yet enter in any real sense at all. In order to answer such a claim, we will first consider the writer's presentation of the two compartments of the tabernacle, then we will consider the vital statement in 10:19 that we now 'have confidence to enter the holy places by the blood of Jesus' (ESV).

The two compartments in the tabernacle

On getting the technical terms right
Our first task is to get clear in our minds the meaning of the technical terms used in chapters 9 and 10 in connection with the tabernacle building. Because of certain translational difficulties the task is not quite so easy as might be expected.

'Even the first covenant had regulations for worship and the earthly holy (place)' (9:1). Here 'the earthly holy place' seems to refer to the whole building. To avoid confusion later on, let's agree to call the holy place in this sense, the sanctuary, on the clear understanding that it refers to the whole building.

The next six verses (9:2–7) tell us two things. First, this sanctuary was divided into two distinctly separate compartments by means of 'the second veil, or curtain'. (It is called 'second' to distinguish it from the first curtain that hung at the entrance to the building: see Exod. 26:36–37 and contrast Exod. 26:31–35).

Second, these two compartments are called 'the first tabernacle' (9:2, 6) and 'the second tabernacle' (9:7). It is important to realize that the term 'the first tabernacle' does not refer to the Mosaic tabernacle as distinct from later successors. 'The first tabernacle' and 'the second tabernacle' were both parts of the Mosaic tabernacle.

The first tabernacle. It is difficult to translate the name of this first tabernacle into acceptable English. In Greek the word is *hagia* which is the neuter plural of the Greek word for 'holy'. Literally translated it would be 'holies'.[2] But plural though it is, it denotes only one place, not two or more: it is the name of the first tabernacle, that is, the first compartment in the Mosaic sanctuary. There was only one such place. In English it would be misleading to translate it by a plural, 'holy places'.[3]

In confirmation we may cite 1 Kings 8:8. The context tells how the priests brought the ark into the Most Holy Place in Solomon's temple. Then verse 8 adds: 'the poles [by which the ark was carried] were so long that the ends of the poles were seen from the Holy Place *before* the Most Holy Place.' In the Greek of the LXX the word used for 'the Holy Place' is once more the plural of the Greek for

2. Cf. Brooke Foss Westcott, *The Epistle to the Hebrews: The Greek Text with Notes and Essays* (London: Macmillan and Co., 1889), p. 245.

3. It is conceivable, though perhaps unlikely, that the neuter plural means 'the holy things' as distinct from the 'most holy things' which were in the second tabernacle.

'holy'. But it would be misleading to translate it by a plural, 'holy places'. It is talking of the counterpart in Solomon's temple of the 'first tabernacle', the first compartment, in the Mosaic sanctuary. There was only one such Holy Place.

The second tabernacle. In some English translations this second compartment is named the 'Holy of Holies', which is a literal rendering of what in Hebrew is a superlative. Hence other English translations use an English superlative: 'the Most Holy Place'. But in the Greek of Hebrews 9:3 the first element in the name is once more a neuter plural: 'Holies of Holies'. (Here too it seems to be following the LXX usage in passages like 1 Kgs 8:6; 2 Chr. 4:22; 5:7.) But in English it would again be misleading to translate it the 'Most Holy Places'. There was only one such Most Holy Place in Moses' sanctuary, or, indeed, in Solomon's, Ezra's or Herod's temples.

One further detail

In the Old Testament, when it is obvious to which compartment in the sanctuary a passage is referring, Scripture will sometimes use the term, 'the Holy Place', to refer in fact to 'the Most Holy Place'. Leviticus 16 is a notable example. In verse 2 of that chapter Aaron is warned not to come at all times into 'the holy place within the veil'. The phrase 'within the veil' immediately determines which holy place this is: it is the Most Holy Place. But having established this, the rest of the chapter happily uses the term 'the Holy Place', to refer to 'the Most Holy Place' (vv. 16, 17, 20). This may serve to remind us always to interpret the meaning of these technical terms in the light of the context in which they occur. If, then, a translation used the term 'holy place' in contexts where there is no initial indication that it is referring to 'the holy place within the veil', this might well confuse the reader.

Why Christian preachers and congregations need to get these technical terms right

Hebrews 9:8–10 tells us that it was the Holy Spirit's design that the Mosaic tabernacle should be composed of two distinct compartments separated by the veil; and secondly that the Holy Spirit designed this symbolism to be a vivid illustration of: (a) where Christ is now since his resurrection and ascension, and (b) the access to God that a believer now has.

Four passages in chapters 9 and 10 contribute to these all-important themes. Let us examine each of them in turn, remembering what (as best as we can make out) the early verses have told us about the two compartments in Moses' tabernacle. And then, not to be unduly critical, but for the sake of clear preaching and teaching, we shall examine what various translations have made of these technical terms. What we have to remember is:

1. The first tabernacle = the first compartment, is called 'the Holies' or 'the Holy Place'.
2. The second tabernacle = the second compartment, is called 'the Holies of Holies', or 'the Most Holy Place'.
3. No-one was allowed to enter the Most Holy Place except the high priest, and he on only one day in the year.

First passage: Hebrews 9:8

> The Holy Ghost this signifying that the way into the holiest of all was not yet made manifest, while as the first tabernacle was yet standing (KJV)

What does 'the first tabernacle' mean in this verse? The same as in verse 2, that is, the first compartment? Or something else? Some scholars say it is something else. F. F. Bruce comments ' . . . whereas hitherto our author has used "the first tabernacle" of the outer compartment of the sanctuary, here he uses it to mean the sanctuary of "the first covenant", comprising holy place and holy of holies together. And here we are to understand not merely the Mosaic tabernacle, but the other structures which replace it from time to time, down to and including Herod's temple'.[4]

---

4. F. F. Bruce, *The Epistle to the Hebrews*, NICNT (Grand Rapids: Eerdmans, 1964), pp. 194–195.

Other scholars, notably Westcott and Moffatt, take the term 'the first tabernacle' in 9:8 to mean the same as it does in the earlier verses 2 and 6, namely the first compartment of the Mosaic sanctuary. This has at least the advantage of consistency in the use of technical terms within the space of a few verses.

Moreover it makes good sense of the phrase at the end of the verse, which the KJV, quoted above, translates: 'while as the first tabernacle was yet standing'. This phrase deserves a more exact translation. To bring out its force Westcott uses a paraphrase: 'while the first tabernacle still has an appointed place answering to a Divine order'.[5] F. F. Bruce suggests 'while the first tabernacle retains its status'.[6]

If then we allow the term 'the first tabernacle' in verse 8 to mean the same as in verses 2 and 6 (which Bruce does not allow), we can rephrase the KJV's translation of verse 8 as: 'the way into the holiest of all has not yet been made manifest while the first tabernacle still has separate status.' Obviously not! What gave the first tabernacle, the Holy Place, its separate status from the Most Holy Place was the veil. For anyone standing in the Holy Place the veil shut out all sight of the Most Holy Place. There was no visible way into the Most Holy Place. This was deliberate on the part of the Holy Spirit, because of the inadequacy of Israel's sacrifices and rituals (9:9–10).

Take away the veil, however, and the Holy Place would no longer have separate status from the Most Holy Place. Simultaneously the way into the Most Holy Place would be open and obvious (Heb. 10:19 will tell us how the veil was removed).

Second passage: Hebrews 9:12

Here Hebrews continues to use tabernacle terminology but uses it of 'the greater and more perfect tabernacle, not made with hands', that is 'the true tabernacle' (8:2), or 'heaven itself'. But again translations diverge. Christ entered once for all into: 'the holy place' (RV,

5. Westcott, *Hebrews*, p. 252.

6. Bruce, *Hebrews*, p. 192, n. 48.

NASB), 'the holy places' (ESV), 'the Holy Place' (RSV). These versions seem to have felt the need to translate the Greek literalistically. But only the ESV fully represents the plural in the Greek, which has *eis ta hagia* (neuter plural). The NEB both here and above at verse 8 uses the term 'sanctuary', seemingly intending to refer to the Most Holy Place. Two other translations indicate their judgment as to what the Greek refers to (as distinct from what it may appear to say): 'the Most Holy Place' (NIV, NKJV).

Third passage: Hebrews 9:24–25

Here we have two verses that may finally help us to make up our minds about the meaning of the technical terms which the New Testament Greek uses in connection with the tabernacle.

We start with verse 25, which explicitly speaks of the *annual* entry of the high priest, that is his once-a-year entry, into the Most Holy Place. That entry has already been referred to in 9:7, and there it is said to be into 'the *second* tabernacle'. There can be no doubt, therefore, about which tabernacle, the first or the second, Hebrews 9:25 is talking about when it refers to the high priest's annual entry: it is the Holy Place within the veil, that is the Most Holy Place.[7] Aaron, Israel's high priest, had to enter the first tabernacle, the Holy Place, every day of the week to burn incense on the golden altar (Exod. 30:7). It is in contrast to these constant entrances that Hebrews 9:25 mentions Aaron's once-a-year entry into the Most Holy Place (see again 9:6–7).[8]

When Aaron entered the Most Holy Place on the Day of Atonement, God 'appeared in the cloud upon the mercy seat' (Lev. 16:2). In that limited sense, Aaron appeared in the presence of God. By contrast verse 24 says that Christ has not entered into holy places

---

7. Even though the Greek of the New Testament at this point uses the phrase *eis ta hagia*: 'into the holies'.

8. Into where then do the various translations of Heb. 9:25 say that Aaron entered on the once-yearly Day of Atonement? Once more some of them are, from the reader's point of view, inadequate: 'the holy places' (ESV), 'the holy place' (RV, NASB, KJV).

made by (human) hands, but into heaven itself, now to appear in the presence of God for us. This undoubtedly is *the* Most Holy Place, the immediate presence of God.

Fourth passage: Hebrews 10:19–20
The Greek, literally translated, says 'boldness to enter "the holies"'. There is no doubt which compartment of the tabernacle, the first or the second, symbolically represents the place we are entitled to enter: it is the second tabernacle, representing the Most Holy Place, the immediate presence of God. We may be sure of this, since verse 20 specifies it as being 'through the veil'. Perhaps that is why some versions (such as RV, NASB) are content to follow the Hebrew of Leviticus 16 and call it simply 'the holy place', because the phrase 'through the veil' indicates which holy place it is. Some versions make sure their English readers realize which holy place it is, by rendering it 'the holiest' (KJV, NKJV) or 'the Most Holy Place' (NIV), or 'the sanctuary' (RSV, NEB) – presumably meaning the heavenly equivalent not of the whole tabernacle, but of the second tabernacle. But once more the ESV by its literalistic translation, 'the holy places' in the plural, might cause confusion in some readers.

The two compartments: a summary
Hebrews 9:1–7 makes unmistakably clear the difference between the first tabernacle and the second, between the Holy Place and the Most Holy Place. Subsequently, however, it uses a variety of terms to denote the Most Holy Place. At 9:8, for instance, it uses the expression 'the way of [or, into] the holy places', where the context shows quite clearly that the phrase 'the holy places' refers in fact to the Most Holy Place. Similarly 9:25 refers to Aaron's yearly entrance into the Most Holy Place, yet it refers to it simply as 'the holy places'. Similarly again, 10:19–20 talk of the new and living way that Christ has inaugurated for us through the veil; yet the phrase they use is 'entrance into the holy places'.

Now in these and other verses many versions translate the phrase 'holy places' literalistically and leave the reader to decide what the phrase refers to: the holy places, or the Most Holy Place, or both. On the other hand in 10:19–20, where the phrase refers without doubt to the Most Holy Place,[9] some versions, such as the NIV and the NKJV, use a dynamic translation 'the Most Holy Place', seeing that is what the phrase 'holy places' refers to here.

In these and such like verses preachers should be aware of this problem. If they are using a literal version, they will need to point out from the context exactly what division of the tabernacle the phrase 'holy places' is referring to.

Access to God's presence: a disputed interpretation

Many thousands in the Orthodox tradition, for example, seem to hold that Christian access into the presence of God today is very little different from what it was for Israel's priests in the tabernacle. The internal design of Orthodox churches copies that of the Old Testament tabernacle. Two thirds of the way down each church there is a high wall extending from one side to the other. In that wall there are three doors. During the liturgy the middle door is open; but only the officiating priest and his assistants are allowed inside. The space inside is seen to be the equivalent of the Most Holy Place in the tabernacle, and the people are not allowed entrance. They have to remain outside. And if the people are not allowed into the Most Holy Place in a church building on earth, they can scarcely think that they already have spiritual access into the immediate presence of God in heaven.

Thousands more – and this time not just Orthodox people – would dispute the NIV's translation of Hebrews 10:19: '. . . confidence *to enter* the Most Holy Place'. The dispute turns on the intended meaning of the Greek word *eisodos* as used in this verse. Like the English 'entrance', *eisodos* can mean two different things according to its context:

---

9. Compare 10:19 with 9:24.

1. a door, or gate, into some building or area; or
2. the actual process of entering that building or area.[10]

Those who favour the first meaning understand Hebrews 10:19 as saying that there is a veil that hides heaven from us; and through that veil we cannot yet enter in any real sense of the term, while we are still on earth. But as towards the end of life we approach the doorway into heaven, we may have every confidence that we shall finally be allowed actually to enter in. If the first meaning were the intended one in Hebrews 10:19, we could paraphrase the verse: boldness, or confidence, as we stand at the entrance, even though at present we are unable, or not allowed, actually to enter.

Those on the other hand who understand *eisodos* as carrying the second meaning would agree that there is a veil that hides heaven from us, and through which we cannot pass physically as long as we are on earth. Yet even now we can enter spiritually into the Most Holy Place, into the immediate presence of God, and come boldly to his throne of grace (4:16).

Which, then, is the intended meaning of *eisodos* in Hebrews 10:19: the doorway into the presence of God? Or, actually entering the presence of God?[11] And how shall we decide? The best way will be to go back to the beginning of this section in Hebrews, and follow the train of thought that begins there.

---

10. An example of the double meaning of the English word 'entrance'. If, confronted by an imposing public building in a foreign city, one asked: 'Where is the entrance?' a local citizen might say: 'See that impressive arched door? That is the entrance.' But if then one tried actually to enter the building, one might be met with a notice: 'Entrance forbidden to all foreigners.'

11. As Thayer/Grimm points out, in the New Testament the word *eisodos* is used only in this second meaning. C. L. W. Grimm, *A Greek-English Lexicon of the New Testament*, tr. and rev. J. H. Thayer (Edinburgh: T. & T. Clark, 2001), p. 188.

The Old Testament priests' access into the tabernacle

Hebrews 9:1–10 points out that the Mosaic tabernacle had two compartments (as we have seen above). The first compartment was called 'the first tabernacle' or 'the Holy Place'. Then after the veil (described as the second veil, to distinguish it from the curtain that hung at the door of the tabernacle) was another compartment, called 'the second tabernacle' (9:7) or 'the Most Holy Place' (in Hebrew 'the Holy of Holies') (9:3). The surrounding verses mention in passing the sacred furniture contained in these two compartments; but their chief concern is with what access the priests had into the Holy Place and then into the Most Holy Place.

We read in 9:6 that 'the priests go in continually into the first tabernacle, accomplishing the services'. We notice the verb 'go in'. They did not stand outside and simply contemplate the door into the Holy Place: they actually entered in.

Similarly with the Most Holy Place. Granted that the ordinary priests were never allowed to go into the Most Holy Place, but only the high priest. Granted also that even the high priest was allowed to go into the Most Holy Place on only one day in the year, the Day of Atonement. Yet on that one day in the year he did actually enter in! Already we are beginning to get a clue to the intended meaning of *eisodos* in 10:19: not merely the doorway into the Most Holy Place, but the actual process of entering the holiest of all.

That said, it must be admitted that access into the Most Holy Place was even for the high priest severely restricted, and for the people totally so. The reason for that was the inadequacy of Israel's sacrifices: they could never perfect the conscience of the worshipper (9:9).[12] But at this point the Holy Spirit sounds a note of hope. Those inadequate sacrifices, he says, were 'only external regulations imposed *until the time of reformation*' (9:9–10). They were only a temporary provision!

---

12. We notice the singular 'worshipper'. Conceivably it might refer simply to the individual high priest. But the same idea is repeated at 10:1–3, and there the plural 'worshippers', is used, making it clear that it refers to all the people.

The implication is clear. When the reformation came, the blood of Christ would 'cleanse the worshippers' conscience from dead works to serve the living God' (9:14). Hence all believers in Christ would have 'hearts sprinkled [that is with the blood of Christ] from an evil conscience and their bodies bathed all over [cf. John 13:10] with pure water' (10:22). Thus cleansed all believers in Christ would be able to do what Israel's high priest could do only once a year in a mere earthly tabernacle: every day of every year every believer would have the confidence actually to enter in spirit into the very presence of the living God in heaven itself, and know himself or herself accepted.

The way into the holiest, then and now

The division of the Mosaic tabernacle by means of a veil into two distinctly separate compartments was deliberate on the part of the Holy Spirit. It conveyed a message (9:8): 'the way into the Most Holy Place was not yet opened up so long as the first tabernacle [that is, the first compartment, the Holy Place] still had separate status.'[13] As noted above, what gave the first tabernacle separate status from the second tabernacle was the veil. As long as it hung there undisturbed, no ordinary priest could see into, let alone enter, the Most Holy Place. Take away the veil, however, and the first tabernacle would cease to have separate status from the second tabernacle. Simultaneously, the way into the Most Holy Place would be completely open.

It was not for nothing, then, that when Christ died on the cross, God had the symbolic veil in the earthly temple torn in two from the top to the bottom (Matt. 27:51). More important still than that symbolic act, is the fact that Christ by his death, resurrection and ascension inaugurated for us a new and living way right into the very presence of God (cf. the term 'access' in Eph. 2:18). We can with confidence enter in.

---

13. For this translation cf. Westcott, *Hebrews*, p. 252.

The significance of the veil

It has customarily been thought that according to Hebrews 10:20 the veil in the tabernacle represented Christ's flesh. But two strong objections have been raised against this view.

The first objection is that Hebrews 6:19–20 says Christ our precursor has entered into 'that which is within the veil'. It would make no sense to say that at his ascension he entered into that which is within his own flesh. That objection, then, is true. But difficulty arises if we fail to distinguish the two different purposes (noted earlier) which the tabernacle was designed to serve.

Purpose one was to be 'a copy and shadow of the heavenly things' (8:5, ESV). For centuries the veil fulfilled this purpose by reminding Israel that human beings could not bodily enter the immediate presence of God (except for one solitary occasion each year on the Day of Atonement). For Israel, then, the veil in the tabernacle (and temple) stood for whatever veil it is that hides the presence of God from our eyes, and forbids our bodily entrance (see by contrast Rev. 6:14–17).

That veil is still in place for us. The wonder of Christ's ascension is that he, a perfect man with a human body, has passed through that veil; and has done so as our precursor (see Acts 1:9–11). We ourselves cannot pass through that veil bodily, nor see through it with our physical eyes. True, when a believer dies, his or her spirit goes from the body and is present with the Lord (2 Cor. 5:6–8). But as far as our bodies are concerned we must await the resurrection at the second coming of Christ (1 Cor. 15:20–23). Until then the veil, in this sense, remains.

But the tabernacle served two purposes, and not just one. It was not just 'a copy and shadow of the heavenly things' for Israelites throughout the centuries before Christ's first coming. For those who live after that coming, the tabernacle, as we now can see, was also designed to be 'a shadow of the good things to come' (10:1, ESV). In contrast to false claimants to be the messiah, the true Messiah, the great reality, is the One who matches and fulfils the shadow. So at this level, just as the animal sacrifices, the lampstand, the table, the incense altar and the mercy-seat were foreshadowings of Christ (whether the ancient Israelites realized it or not), so was the veil, as Hebrews 10:20 states. But here we meet the second strong objection.

The famous commentator, Bishop B. F. Westcott, could not bring himself to think that Scripture would ever say, or even imply, that Christ's flesh acted as a veil, as an obstacle to the vision of God.[14] He suggested, therefore, that the syntax of Hebrews 10:20 should be construed as follows: 'the new and living way which Christ has inaugurated for us through the veil, that is to say, the way of his flesh'; and the NEB in its text follows Westcott's suggestion.

But this objection overlooks the fact that though the veil barred access into the immediate presence of God, it was, for ordinary priests, a merciful provision. Without the veil, the Holy Place and the Most Holy Place would have been one continuous open space. To enter even the Holy Place would then have been to enter the immediate presence of God – a thing impossible for the ordinary priests because of the inadequacy of their sacrifices. As it was, however, the veil allowed them to come to the lampstand, table and incense altar in the Holy Place. They could even come to the veil itself, contemplate its symbolic colours and cherubim, and thus learn something of the glory of the God whose presence filled the Most Holy Place inside the veil.

In this sense the veil beautifully foreshadows Christ 'in the days of his flesh' (Heb. 5:7, ESV). The crowds thronged him; sinful men and women could touch the hem of his garment; a repentant woman washed his feet with her tears, dried them with her hair and anointed them with ointment; little children could nestle in his arms – yet all the while all the fullness of the Godhead dwelt in him bodily. 'We handled him', says John (1 John 1:1); 'we beheld the glory of the Word become flesh' (John 1:14).

The rending of his flesh at Calvary, however, opened up a way for us to see right into the heart of God. Moreover, through him

---

14. Westcott, *Hebrews*, p. 320.

'we both [Jew and Gentile] now have access in one Spirit unto the Father' (Eph. 2:18). Risen and ascended into the very presence of God, he has ceased to act as a veil.

With this we return to the verses 10:19–22 and to the dispute over the meaning of the Greek word *eisodos*: does it mean 'the doorway into the Most Holy Place', or 'the actual process of entering into the Most Holy Place'? Let us sum up the evidence for its right interpretation.

Decisive details in Hebrews 10:19–22

We notice first that the *eisodos* into the Most Holy Place is itself declared to be 'a way', 'a road', 'a path', along which we are to 'draw near', 'approach', 'come to' the immediate presence of God in the Holy of Holies. The *eisodos* is not merely a door.

The *eisodos* is, second, further described as 'a new and living way' that the Lord Jesus initiated for us. It was certainly new compared with the situation in the tabernacle. As we noticed earlier, as long as the veil divided the tabernacle into two distinctly separate compartments, 'the way into the Most Holy Place' was not yet made manifest (9:8). The veil, in fact, barred all entry into the Most Holy Place (except once a year for the high priest). Now, by contrast, actual entry into the immediate presence of God is completely open for all believers along this new way, and they are exhorted to draw near to God.

Finally, our confidence actually to enter into the immediate presence of God in the Most Holy Place in the greater and more perfect tabernacle (9:11), is said to be made possible 'by the blood of Christ' (10:19). The reason why the veil in Moses' tabernacle barred all entry into the Most Holy Place was because the blood of animals and washings in water could not clear the conscience of the worshippers. Moreover the solemn ceremonies of the Day of Atonement taught the people that their very presence round the tabernacle defiled it (Lev. 16:10; Heb. 9:23). But the blood of Christ, by contrast, perfectly cleanses believers' consciences (9:14) so that they are no longer afraid to enter the Presence; and simultaneously the presence in heaven of once-time sinners, now cleansed by the blood of Christ, does not defile heaven itself (9:23; 10:22).

We conclude, therefore, that according to Hebrews 10:19–22 believers in the here and now may actually enter in spirit into the immediate presence of God, and are encouraged confidently to take advantage of this supreme privilege.

A note on the golden altar of incense

Hebrews 9:4 appears to say that the golden altar of incense stood in the Most Holy Place. Exodus 30:6–8, however, makes it clear that it stood, not in the Most Holy Place, but in the Holy Place. It could not have stood in the Most Holy Place, for Aaron was required to burn incense on it, morning and evening, every day of the year, which he could not have done had it stood in the Most Holy Place. On the other hand, Exodus 30:6 specifies that it must stand 'before the veil that is by the ark of the testimony, before the mercy-seat that is over the testimony, where I will meet with you'. In other words, though it stood outside the veil in the Holy Place, it had a functional relationship with the ark and the mercy-seat, and indeed with God who met with Moses there. This is why 1 Kings 6:22 refers to the incense altar as '*belonging to* the oracle' (i.e. the inner compartment which contained the ark), even though it makes it clear that this altar stood outside in the Holy Place. If I said 'my house has a garage', no one would think that it necessarily stood inside my house. In that sense, the Most Holy Place had the altar of incense.

Conclusion: a tabernacle pattern

Hebrews is insistent on the superiority of the sacrifice of Christ to the Old Testament sacrifices in general, and in particular to the sacrifices which cleansed the tabernacle on the yearly Day of Atonement (9:11–14, 23–24). Once we have grasped this difference, however, the rituals on the Day of Atonement provide us with a pattern that beautifully illustrates what Christ has done, and will yet do, for us.

On the Day of Atonement the Aaronic high priest made three appearances to make atonement for the sin of the people (Lev. 16:15–22).[15]

1. First he appeared before the people in the open court of the tabernacle; selected a goat as a sin-offering for the people; its blood was shed, and caught in a bowl (16:15).
2. Then the high priest took the blood into the Most Holy Place and appeared in the presence of God for and on behalf of the people as their representative, sprinkling the blood before and on the mercy-seat (16:15–16).
3. Then he came out again and appeared the second time before the people, took a second goat, and over its head confessed the nation's sins; and the goat was then driven away into the wilderness (16:20–22).

Similarly Christ's atoning work for us involves three appearances:

1. 'He has appeared once for all at the end of the ages to put away sin by the sacrifices of himself' (Heb. 9:26, ESV).
2. 'Christ has entered . . . into heaven itself, now to appear in the presence of God on our behalf' (9:24, ESV).
3. 'Christ, having been offered once to bear the sins of many, will appear a second time, not to deal with sin, but to save those who are eagerly waiting for him' (Heb. 9:28, ESV).

All Christ's three appearances are exceedingly wonderful; but perhaps the second of them is, for us in our present state,

---

15. The earlier appearance in which Aaron presents a sacrifice to deal with his own sin and the sin of his priestly house (Lev. 16:11–14) is, of course, unnecessary in the case of Jesus' high priestly work (cf. Heb. 7:27; 9:7).

particularly comforting. That the Son of God should return to heaven from which he came is surely to be expected. What is astonishing is that he appears in the presence of God *for us*, as our forerunner and representative. God is aware, of course, that Christ represents all of us who trust him. In accepting him, therefore, God accepts us. In that confidence we can enter his presence.

© David Gooding, 2012

5. WARNING AND ASSURANCE

RUN THE RACE TO THE END

Thomas R. Schreiner

Hebrews seems like a strange and forbidding book for those who have not read the Bible frequently or for those who are relatively new to reading the Bible. But the one passage from Hebrews they often know is the incredibly strong warning in Hebrews 6:4–8. Indeed, it is quite likely that they have been involved in a vigorous argument over what these verses mean and whether believers could lose their salvation. Popular debates over Hebrews 6:4–8 reflect the state of scholarship as well, as scholars have long disagreed on how we should interpret the warnings found in the letter. My fundamental purpose in this essay is to unfold the meaning of these warning texts. I will briefly, however, sketch in other interpretations and interact with some of them while presenting my own view.

It is important to note that Hebrews is permeated with warnings, and hence a convincing interpretation of 6:4–8 must interact with the other admonitions in the letter. First and foremost Hebrews is a sermon (13:22), and hence the purpose of the letter is found in the exhortations given to the readers. The elegant and profound theology of the letter serves the warnings, with the result that the import of the admonitions is deepened by the profound theology that undergirds them. The precise parameters of the warning passages are disputed among scholars. The interpretation proposed here does not depend upon identifying precisely where the texts begin and end. In this essay I am delineating 2:1–4; 3:7 – 4:13; 5:11 – 6:12; 10:26–31 and 12:25–29 as the warning passages. As Scot McKnight rightly insists in his excellent essay, the warnings in the letter must be interpreted together because the passages cast light upon one another.[1] The warnings should be interpreted *synoptically*. Remarkably, interpreters have often violated this insight and have isolated 6:4–8 as if it were the only admonition in the letter. Such an approach is flawed, for the author in his sermon drives home one main point: don't fall away! He expresses this point in a diversity of ways in the various warning passages. Therefore, these passages are like a kaleidoscope which present the same issue from a number of different angles.

Before embarking upon an interpretation of the various warning passages it should prove helpful to note the main interpretations of the warning texts throughout history. The purpose here is not to include all the interpretations offered but to cite those which have had a significant impact upon the church. First, Arminians understand the admonitions to be addressed to genuine believers, who are warned that if they commit apostasy and fall away from the Lord, then they are guilty of abandoning the salvation they once enjoyed. Arminians argue, therefore, that true believers may forsake their salvation.[2] Second, others maintain (I will call it the 'fruitful view') that the warnings are addressed to true believers, but the sin in view

---

1. Scot McKnight, 'The Warning Passages of Hebrews: A Formal Analysis and Theological Conclusions', *TJ* 13 (1992), pp. 21–59.

2. So McKnight, 'Warning Passages', pp. 21–59; Grant R. Osborne, 'A Classical Arminian View', in Herbert W. Bateman IV (ed.), *Four Views on the Warning Passages in Hebrews* (Grand Rapids: Kregel, 2007), pp. 86–128; Gareth Lee Cockerill, 'A Wesleyan Arminian View', in Bateman, *Four Views*, pp. 257–292.

is not apostasy.[3] Believers are exhorted to follow the Lord in true discipleship. If they fail to heed the warnings, they will not lose their salvation, for no one truly called by the Lord can apostatize. What they will miss out on, though, is a joyful Christian life where they bear fruit as Christians. Third, another interpretation, which could be labelled the 'almost Christians' view, maintains that the warnings are not addressed to those who are truly believers.[4] Those described in 6:4–5 are close to being believers but are not truly saved.

It might be helpful to note agreements and disagreements among the various interpretations. All the interpretations except the 'almost Christians' view maintain that the warnings are directed to Christians. The Arminian reading concludes that true Christians can apostatize and lose a salvation they once had, whereas the 'fruitful view' and the 'almost Christians' view argue that true believers will never apostatize. All the views, except the 'fruitful view', argue that the

---

3. The best representative of this view is Randall C. Gleason, 'A Moderate Reformed View', in Bateman, *Four Views*, pp. 336–377. For this view in general, see Charles Stanley, *Eternal Security: Can You Be Sure?* (Nashville: Thomas Nelson, 1990); R. T. Kendall, *Once Saved, Always Saved* (Chicago: Moody Press, 1983); Zane C. Hodges, *The Gospel Under Siege: A Study on Faith and Works* (Dallas: Redención Viva, 1981); idem, *Absolutely Free: A Biblical Reply to Lordship Salvation* (Grand Rapids: Zondervan, 1989); Michael Eaton, *No Condemnation: A New Theology of Assurance* (Downers Grove: IVP, 1995).

4. So John Owen, *Hebrews: The Epistle of Warning* (Grand Rapids: Kregel, 1953), pp. 96–98. This work is an abridgement by M. J. Tryon of John Owen's *Exposition of the Epistle to the Hebrews* originally published in eight volumes (1670s); Roger Nicole, 'Some Comments on Hebrews 6:4–6 and the Doctrine of the Perseverance of God with the Saints', in Gerald F. Hawthorne (ed.), *Current Issues in Biblical and Patristic Interpretation: Studies in Honor of Merrill C. Tenney Presented by His Former Students* (Grand Rapids: Eerdmans, 1975), pp. 355–364; Wayne Grudem, 'Perseverance of the Saints: A Case Study from the Warning Passages in Hebrews', in Thomas R. Schreiner and Bruce A. Ware (eds.), *Still Sovereign* (Grand Rapids: Baker, 2000), pp. 133–182; Buist M. Fanning, 'A Classical Reformed View,' in Bateman, *Four Views*, pp. 172–219.

punishment for falling away is damnation. The 'fruitful view' argues that believers will lose out on rewards and joy in this life, but they will still be saved even if they do not heed the warnings.

My goal in the remainder of the chapter is to survey the warning texts in Hebrews. I will argue that the warnings are addressed to genuine believers, that the threat is eternal damnation, and that it is illegitimate to conclude from the warnings that true believers may fall away, for the texts examined here are warnings and admonitions, not declarations. The warnings should be understood as *the means* by which true believers are preserved from apostasy. It is imperative to see, then, that the warnings are *prospective* and not *retrospective*. Their function is to urge readers to persevere in both faith and obedience to Jesus Christ.

Hebrews 2:1–4

The warning in 2:1–4 is brief, and we will concentrate here on verses 1–3. It is certainly addressed to believers, and the author includes himself, using 'we' explicitly in both verses 1 and 3. The sin they are cautioned against is described in three ways: failing to pay attention to what they heard at the beginning (v. 1); drifting or slipping away from the gospel (v. 1); and 'neglect[ing] such a great salvation' (v. 3). The terms used here are ambiguous. They could signify apostasy or designate sin that is less momentous.

There are two reasons for thinking that apostasy is in view. First, we shall see that the language used in most of the other warning passages suggests radical departure from the Christian faith. Second, the punishment delineated here almost certainly refers to eschatological judgment. Such a conclusion is supported by the argument in verses 2–3. The author argues from the lesser to the greater. If Israel under the law was punished for its infractions of what God prescribed, then surely believers will not escape retribution if they 'neglect such a great salvation' (v. 3). The penalty for drifting away is more significant than the earthly punishment Israel endured, and hence it most likely refers to eschatological judgment. The verb 'escape' (*ekpheugō*) occurs eight times in the New Testament, and in five of them refers to escaping final judgment (Luke 21:36; Rom. 2:3; 1 Thess. 5:3; Heb. 2:3; 12:25). The parallel in Hebrews 12 is particularly instructive, for the author (see exegesis below) argues from the lesser to the greater, as he does in chapter 2, and almost certainly has in mind final judgment.[5] Hence, the readers are urged not to drift away from or neglect the salvation that they enjoy, for God will judge those who do not remain faithful.

Hebrews 3:7 – 4:13

The warning here is quite long, as the author cites part of Psalm 95 and applies it to his readers. I will ask again the three questions that were posed in the previous passage. To whom is the warning addressed? It is clearly addressed to believers. They are identified as 'brothers' (v. 12) and as 'any of you' (v. 12); they are to 'exhort one another' (v. 13); are spoken of as 'none of you' (v. 13) and 'any of you' (4:1; cf. 4:7). The writer again includes himself among those needing the warning: 'let us fear' (4:1); 'us' (4:2); 'let us therefore strive to enter that rest' (4:11; cf. 3:14).

What is the nature of the warning given to the believers? They must not harden their hearts and rebel against the Lord (3:8, 15; 4:7) or test the Lord (3:9). The sin is described as going 'astray in their heart' (3:10) or as disobedience (3:18; 4:6, 11). More specifically, the writer cautions the readers against having 'an evil, unbelieving heart' and warns them not 'to fall away from the living God' (3:12, 19; 4:2, 3) or to 'be hardened by the deceitfulness of sin' (3:13). It seems quite clear that the sin warned against here is apostasy, for the author warns his readers specifically about the danger of falling away (3:12). He is not merely cautioning them against temporary unbelief or

---

5. Nevertheless, if 2:1–4 were the only warning passage, the nature of the penalty would be difficult to discern.

rebellion, but a definitive hardening of the heart against the Lord, so that they no longer trust in him and obey him. They must not follow the example of Israel in the wilderness who failed to trust in and obey the Lord.

What will be the consequence of the believers falling away? The author warns them repeatedly that they will not enter God's rest (3:11, 18, 19; 4:1, 3, 5, 6, 8, 9, 11). Israel failed to enter the rest of the Promised Land because of her disobedience and rebellion. The rest promised to the people of God is greater than residing in the land of Canaan. God promises them a heavenly city (11:10, 14–16; 13:14). The danger of not entering the rest confirms that the sin in view is apostasy, for those who harden their hearts and fail to believe will not enjoy the heavenly inheritance and will not enter the heavenly city. They will miss out on the Sabbath rest God has promised his people (4:9). It seems quite clear that the author refers here to eschatological salvation in terms of rest, and hence those who do not enter God's rest will experience eschatological judgment. This confirms the notion that apostasy is the danger that must be avoided.

Fanning, who supports the 'almost Christians' view, raises an objection to the reading proposed here, for he understands the conditional statements in 3:6 and 3:14 to say that the Hebrews were already members of the people of God so that endurance to the end functions as evidence that they were saved.[6] He maintains that the conditions here do not designate a cause-effect relationship but an evidence-to-inference relationship. The author, according to Fanning, is not presenting a condition which one must meet to be saved on the final day. Rather, perseverance simply functions as evidence, says Fanning, that they were already saved. Whether some conditions should be identified as evidence to inference, as Fanning proposes, warrants more discussion than is possible here. Even if one agrees that some conditions should be construed as evidence to inference, it is more natural to read the conditions in 3:6 and 3:14 as presenting a contingent situation, so the author is saying that the

---

6. Fanning, 'Classical Reformed', pp. 206–218.

readers must persevere to the end to be saved. Fanning turns the conditions in 3:6 and 3:14 into retrospective reflections. The major problem with Fanning's view is that the other conditional statements in Hebrews are prospective, and thus it is quite unlikely that the conditions in Hebrews 3:6 and 3:14 would function differently from the other conditions in the letter.[7] Here the interpretive principle stated at the beginning of the chapter comes into play. The warning passages are all designed to underscore the importance of perseverance until the end to obtain eschatological salvation. It is quite unlikely that two conditions in the letter (3:6, 14) should be interpreted in a different manner from the other conditional statements in the letter.

Hebrews 5:11 – 6:12

Certainly the most famous warning passage is 5:11 – 6:12, and it has been the subject of considerable controversy. To whom are the warnings addressed? Those who support the 'almost Christians' view contend that those addressed are not genuine believers. Wayne Grudem has written the most extensive defence of this view, and he says that the list in verses 4–5 does not definitively prove that those addressed in Hebrews were saved.[8] Grudem lists eighteen marks of genuine salvation in Hebrews and argues that the experiences noted in 6:4–5 do not clearly match genuine salvation. Some of the eighteen qualities listed by Grudem include forgiveness of sins, cleansing of the conscience, the law written on the heart, a holy life, being pleasing to God, having faith, hope and love, obeying God, persevering, entering God's rest, knowing God, sharing in Christ, etc. Since none of these qualities is attributed to the Hebrews, Grudem avers, they were not clearly saved.

---

7. Rightly Osborne, 'Classical Arminian', p. 231; Cockerill, 'Wesleyan Arminian', pp. 242–244.

8. Grudem, 'Perseverance of the Saints', pp. 162–168.

The notion that the readers are described as 'almost Christians' is unconvincing. The admonition is clearly addressed to the readers, as the second person plural pronouns attest (see 5:11, 12; 6:9, 10, 11, 12), and once again the author includes himself as well (6:1). The fivefold description of the readers in verses 4–5 most naturally refers to Christians. The most important piece of evidence is the third item in the list: 'partakers (*metochous*) of the Holy Spirit' (NASB, v. 4). Partaking of the Spirit is the fundamental evidence that one belongs to God. For instance, Paul assures the Galatians that they are truly Christians because they have received the Holy Spirit (Gal. 3:2, 5). Peter uses the same argument at the apostolic council to persuade those present that Gentiles are part of the people of God without being circumcised; God gave Gentiles the Spirit apart from circumcision (Acts 15:7–11). Similarly, Paul teaches that *the* mark that one is a Christian is the indwelling of the Holy Spirit (Rom. 8:9; 1 Cor. 2:6–16). Nor is there any reason to think that the author of Hebrews thinks of a partial or incomplete experience of the Spirit. In the same passage he uses the same root word to speak of 'partaking (*metechōn*) of milk' (5:13).[9] There is no suggestion that the term 'partaking' denotes a partial or incomplete digestion of milk. Similarly, the partaking of the Spirit refers to the reception of the Holy Spirit, which indicates that the author addresses believers. Indeed, it is hard to imagine a clearer description of what it means to be a believer, for believers are distinguished by their reception of the Holy Spirit.

The other items in the list should be understood similarly. 'Those who have once been enlightened' (6:4) could be explained in terms of partial enlightenment, but the parallel in 10:32, where the author refers to the time when the readers 'were enlightened' and suffered for the sake of Christ, suggests that the phrase refers to those who had a saving understanding of the gospel. The tasting of the heavenly gift, the goodness of the word of God and the powers of the age

---

9. The translation here is my own. The author uses the same word to denote full and complete sharing elsewhere. Cf. 2:14; 12:8.

to come (6:4–5) also depict the blessings of new life in Christ. The word 'tasting' (*geusamenos*) does not refer to a mere sipping as if the readers had only preliminary or limited experiences of salvation, for the same word is used of Jesus' tasting (*geusētai*) death (2:9). Obviously, Jesus did not merely sip death but experienced it fully. So too, the tasting of the heavenly gift, the word of God and the powers of the coming age represent the experience of those who belong to the people of God. The author is not trying to subtly describe here those who are not believers. Rather he is giving reasons why the readers should respond to his admonition. Since they have been blessed by God with new life, they should respond accordingly with faith and obedience.

What are the readers warned against in this text? They are admonished because they have become spiritually dull (5:11; 6:12) and are in danger of living unfruitful lives (6:7–8). Hence, they are admonished not to fall away (6:6). Some commentators have interpreted the participle 'falling away' (*parapesontas*) as if the author is making a declaration that the readers *have fallen* away already (6:6).[10] It is precisely here that the synoptic reading of the warning passages is enormously helpful, for it is manifestly clear in all the other warning texts that the author is not making a declaration about the spiritual history of the readers. He *warns* the readers about what will happen *if* they fall away (2:1–4; 3:12 – 4:11; 10:26–31; 12:25–29). Therefore, we have strong reasons for believing that 5:11 – 6:12 should be understood along the same lines. It is quite improbable that the author departs from the other warning passages by actually *declaring* that the readers have fallen away. We must remember that the author of Hebrews wrote the letter for one reason, and all the warning passages contribute to that purpose. He solemnly warns the readers not to depart from Christ and the gospel. It would be

---

10. E.g., Nicole, 'Some comments on Hebrews 6:4–6', p. 355; Osborne, 'Classical Arminian', pp. 112, 114, 116. For recognition that the participle is conditional and should not be read as a declaration, see Cockerill, 'Wesleyan Arminian', pp. 275–276.

quite strange if 5:11 – 6:12 were an exception to this pattern so
that in this text the author tells them that they have already fallen
away![11]

All the interpretations proposed, except for the 'fruitful view',
maintain that 'falling away' here denotes apostasy. That the sin is
apostasy is supported, as we have seen, by 3:12 – 4:13, for the
punishment there is failing to enter God's rest. Such a severe
penalty only makes sense if the sin is a complete rejection of Christ.
The admonition in 5:11 – 6:12 coheres with such an interpretation.
What is envisioned is an incapability to repent (6:6). Repentance
is necessary for *entrance* into the people of God, and the impos-
sibility of repentance signifies that forgiveness will not be granted.
The sin contemplated is not merely a temporary defection but
involves 'crucifying . . . the Son of God' and 'holding him up to
contempt' (6:6). It is difficult to believe that someone who follows
the example of those who crucified and mocked Jesus of Nazareth
could enjoy eschatological salvation. Killing and scorning Jesus do
not represent the behaviour of those who belong to the people
of God. Indeed, the author underscores the outrageousness of
such sin, for if they fall away they are crucifying *the Son of God* all
over again.

The penalty threatened also supports a reference to apostasy.
Some might think the illustration of the land and the fruit points to
the 'fruitful view'. But a careful reading of the text is instructive, for
it is not the fruit that is burned but the land (6:8), which represents
the individuals themselves in the illustration.[12] So, the author does
not contemplate their fruit being burned but the persons who fall
away being burned in the judgment. In the same way, the land (and

---

11. Nor is it plausible to say that he speaks of another group which has
    already fallen away. We noted above that 5:11 – 6:12 is addressed
    specifically to the congregation(s) and the author includes himself in
    the admonition.

12. In describing the punishment in such a way here and in other places in
    the essay I am not suggesting that the readers have actually committed
    apostasy.

therefore those who apostatize) is threatened with a final curse (*kataras*) for being unfruitful (6:8). Confirmation for this reading appears in 6:9, for the author is persuaded about the readers' ultimate 'salvation' (6:9), as he is persuaded that the readers will heed his warning. Naturally this means that if they fail to pay attention to his warning they will not be saved. Only by responding to the warning will they 'inherit the promises' (6:12), suggesting that refusal to believe and obey would lead to final judgment.

One other feature of the warning here must be noted. If the warning is here addressed to Christians, does it follow that genuine believers can apostatize? Many would argue in the affirmative, and we can certainly understand why this conclusion would be drawn. Several crucial observations must be made here, however, which suggest that such a conclusion is mistaken. None of the warning passages teaches that true believers fall away. The texts function as *warnings*, not as *declarations* about the spiritual state of those who fall away. Interpreters are prone to read these texts *retrospectively* as if they designate the spiritual state of those who apostatize, but the texts function *prospectively*. They represent urgent challenges for those travelling to the heavenly city. It is not the author's purpose in the midst of the warning to discuss whether true believers can and do fall away. Whether true believers can apostatize must be determined from the entire canonical witness. I would argue that there are good reasons for concluding that true believers are preserved from apostasy (John 6:37–40; 10:28–30; Rom. 5:9; 8:28–39; 1 Cor. 1:8–9; Phil. 1:6; 1 Thess. 5:24; 1 Pet. 1:5), but such an interpretation cannot be defended here. But we do have a clue in Hebrews that the author believes that his warnings will be a *means* by which the readers are preserved from apostasy. He writes to rouse the readers to action so that they will not be sluggish but will persist in faith until the end (6:11–12), and he is persuaded that they will respond to the warnings in faith and be saved on the last day (6:9). Furthermore, the unchangeable character of God's promises suggests that those who truly belong to the Lord will be preserved until the end (6:13–20).

Hebrews 10:26–31

The warning in 10:26–31 is short but pungent. To whom is the warning addressed? Clearly the author speaks to his readers, and he includes himself in those who must respond ('if *we* go on sinning deliberately', v. 26). It appears that those described in these verses must be Christians since they received knowledge of the truth and are described as sanctified (vv. 26, 29). Grudem argues, however, that receiving the knowledge of the truth (v. 26) is equivalent to being enlightened (6:4) and does not represent a saving knowledge.[13] It means someone has heard and understood the gospel, but it does not follow from this that such people have actually trusted Christ personally. Neither does the word 'sanctified' indicate a reference to believers according to Grudem.[14] He maintains that the word 'sanctify' is often used of outward and ceremonial cleansing in Scripture (Heb. 9:13; 1 Cor. 7:14; Matt. 23:17, 19), concluding that a ceremonial sense is probable here since the author compares the work of Christ with Levitical sacrifices. Therefore, the sanctification in view in Hebrews 10:29 is not a saving sanctification, in Grudem's view, but an outward type of cleansing, which is experienced in hearing the gospel.

Grudem's interpretation is possible but unlikely. 'Knowledge of the truth' (*epignōsis alētheias*) in the Pastorals always refers to experiencing salvation (1 Tim. 2:4; 2 Tim. 2:25; 3:7; Titus 1:1). It seems likely that it has the same meaning in Hebrews. Elsewhere in the New Testament 'the truth' often refers to the gospel (e.g., Gal. 2:5, 14; 5:7; Eph. 1:13; Col. 1:5; 2 Thess. 2:10, 12, 13; 2 Tim. 2:15, 18; 3:8; 4:4; Titus 1:14; Jas 1:18; 5:19; 1 Pet. 1:22; 1 John 1:6). Receiving 'the knowledge of the truth' seems to be a natural way to designate embracing the Christian faith. Nor is it likely that the sanctification in 10:29 is merely external. The contrast with Levitical sanctification is intended to emphasize the superiority of Christ's work, for the sanctification accomplished by Christ is effective and internal in

---

13. Grudem, 'Perseverance of the Saints', pp. 176–177.
14. Ibid., pp. 177–178.

contrast to Levitical sanctification. Throughout Hebrews the old covenant outwardly symbolizes what is now an inward reality through Christ. Grudem, by relegating the sanctification in 10:29 to ceremonial sanctification actually contravenes one of the major themes of Hebrews – what was anticipated in shadowy form in the Old Testament has now become a reality in and through the sacrifice of Christ. Strangely, he equates what Christ has done with Old Testament sacrifices, when the point of the author is precisely the opposite. Christ's sacrifice, contrary to the sacrifices offered under the old covenant, is not merely outward or ceremonial (7:1 – 10:18).

We also have good reasons for thinking that the sin in view is apostasy, for the author speaks of 'sinning deliberately' (v. 26). Such sin matches sinning presumptuously in the Old Testament where there is no forgiveness for such rebellion (e.g., Num. 15:30; Deut. 17:12; Ps. 19:13). Apparently the sin envisioned here is a rejection of and rebellion against the Christ. Verse 29 confirms such an interpretation. God will punish those severely who trample underfoot the Son of God, who consider the blood shed by Christ to be unclean, and who insult the Holy Spirit who grants grace. I find it impossible to believe that anything other than apostasy is in view when the author describes trampling Jesus under one's feet, rejecting his blood as unclean and insulting the Holy Spirit! The language is strikingly similar to 6:6, and both texts confirm that ordinary sin is not envisioned.[15] Furthermore, if we interpret all of the warning passages synoptically, it is quite clear that the issue is apostasy in all the texts. The author admonishes the readers not to turn away from the gospel they initially received.

Support for understanding the sin as apostasy is found in the consequences threatened for those who deliberately sin. In previous texts the author threatens readers with no escape if they turn away (2:3), with exclusion from the heavenly rest (3:11, 18, 19; 4:1, 3, 5, 6, 8, 9, 11), and with a curse and burning (6:7–8). We already saw that

---

15. I am not minimizing any sin in saying this. I am only pointing out that we have a definitive and final rejection of the Son of God in this text.

there are solid reasons to understand all these to refer to final judgment, and that reading is more than confirmed by 10:26. If the readers reject the atonement of Christ, whom the author has set forth as the Melchizedekian priest who has offered the final and definitive sacrifice for sins (7:1 – 10:18), they will not be forgiven their sins. No animal sacrifice can provide such forgiveness now that Christ has come. And if those who turn away from Christ cannot be forgiven, then they will be judged on the last day. The author drives home in subsequent verses the impending judgment for those who apostatize. There will be 'fearful expectation of judgment, and a fury of fire that will consume the adversaries' (v. 27). The ferocity of the language rules out merely losing rewards; eternal judgment is obviously described. The author picks up the theme we saw in the first two warning passages (2:1–4; 3:12 – 4:13), where Israel's earthly judgment functions as a type of the judgment to come (vv. 28–29). But the point is that the judgment is escalated from the fulfilment to the type, so that now the judgment is final and definitive, so that those who are judged are excluded from the heavenly city (11:10, 14–16; 13:14). God will inflict his vengeance on those who depart from him and judge them, just as he did Israel of old (Deut. 32:35). It passes all understanding to think that the author refers only to loss of rewards when he says: 'It is a fearful thing to fall into the hands of the living God' (v. 31). He clearly threatens them with final judgment. One final comment should be made about this text. The great 'faith' chapter (11:1–40) illustrates what it means to persevere. The antonym to apostasy is faith that leads to obedience, and clearly Jesus Christ functions as the supreme exemplar here (12:1–4).

Hebrews 12:25–29

The last warning passage is quite brief, and in this way forms a nice *inclusio* with the first one (2:1–4). We see further evidence that the admonitions are directed to believers, for the writer addresses the readers directly ('See that you do not refuse', v. 25), and also includes himself among those who need to heed the warning ('we', v. 25; 'let us', twice in v. 28; and 'our God', v. 29). The sin is described as 'refusing' him (v. 25). But by this stage of the letter we know from the other warnings that the refusal is no minor matter, that it represents a definitive turning away and rejection of the Son of God. The author also picks up the typological relationship between the church and Israel in contemplating the punishment threatened, and we have seen this parallel quite clearly in 2:1–4, 3:12 – 4:13 and 10:26–31. If Israel was not spared when they rejected the Lord on the way to the land of promise, neither will believers be spared, since now the final and definitive revelation (1:2) comes from heaven (vv. 25–27). The threat of the final verse, 'for our God is a consuming fire' (v. 29), reminds us of the terrifying language in 10:31. Surely, the punishment envisioned here is eschatological judgment.

Conclusion

I have argued through a 'synoptic' reading of the warning passages in Hebrews that the author addresses believers, that the sin he warns them against is apostasy (turning away finally and definitively from Christ), and that the punishment threatened refers to the final judgment. In many ways, then, I am closest to the Arminian reading of the passage. The difference, however, is that a canonical reading of the New Testament (see above) teaches that genuine believers will not apostatize. God will continue the good work he started in us (Phil. 1:6). Indeed, the emphasis on the perfection accomplished by Christ (see esp. 10:14) and the theme of the new covenant where the law is written irrevocably on the heart (8:6–13; 10:15–18) indicates that God's saving work will not be undone in those who are his own.[16]

---

16. One of my PhD students at the Southern Baptist Theological Seminary, Chris Cowan, is working on the theme of assurance in Hebrews, which has been neglected in scholarship. His forthcoming work is titled, *'Confident of Better Things': Assurance of Salvation in the Letter to the Hebrews.*

Many object that there is no use giving warnings to those who are unable to apostatize. Several things may be said in reply. First, warnings function *prospectively*, not *retrospectively*. They are instructions shouted out to runners in the race, not armchair reflections on the race subsequent to the action. That leads me to a second observation. The warnings still have a function: they are a *means* by which God preserves believers from falling. When Jesus admonishes his disciples not to deny him or he will deny them (Matt. 10:32–33), his stern words are one motivation for not repudiating Jesus.

Third, another common objection is that the author did not *know* if all those addressed were truly believers. He was not given infallible knowledge that all those addressed would persevere. A couple of things must be said in reply. Our first job as interpreters is to pay attention to the text. We have seen that there are decisive reasons for thinking that the author addresses *believers*. Hence, the function of the text is not to consider the state of those who fall away. Other texts provide that perspective (cf. 1 John 2:19). If the strong warnings in Hebrews are addressed only to those who are almost Christians, then it isn't our mail! But the text precludes such a reading. The author addresses believers explicitly. But that returns us to our objection. Was the author claiming that every single recipient of the letter was regenerate, or that all without exception would respond positively to the warnings? I would suggest that we are now asking a question that the author of Hebrews does not answer. He warns and admonishes, and does not resolve specifically the question we are asking. But I suspect he would answer that he was generalizing, for he was addressing the congregation(s) as a whole. He does not pause to consider the question whether some in the congregation were not truly believers, for that would distract from his purpose. His admonitions were for believers and he expected his warnings to provoke those whom he addressed to faith and obedience. But if the author were asked, 'What about those who fall away?' I think he would agree with John. 'They never belonged to us.'[17] I think it is fitting to conclude with the words of Herman Bavinck, for he captures the function of the warnings in Hebrews wonderfully.

Now the question with respect to this doctrine of perseverance is not whether those who have obtained a true saving faith could not, if left to themselves, lose it again by their own fault and sins: nor whether sometimes all the activity, boldness, and comfort of faith, actually ceases, and faith itself goes into hiding under the cares of life and the delights of the world. The question is whether God upholds, continues, and completes the work of grace he has begun, or whether he sometimes permits it to be totally ruined by the power of sin. Perseverance . . . is a gift of God . . . He watches over it and sees to it that the work of grace is continued and completed. He does not, however, do this apart from believers but through them. In regeneration and faith, he grants a grace that as such bears an inadmissible character; he grants a life that is by nature eternal; he bestows the benefits of calling, justification, and glorification that are mutually and unbreakably interconnected. All of the above-mentioned admonitions and threats that Scripture addresses to believers, therefore, do not prove a thing against the doctrine of perseverance. They are rather the way in which God himself confirms his promise and gift through believers. They are the means by which perseverance in life is realized. After all, perseverance is also not coercive but, as a gift of God, impacts humans in a spiritual manner. It is precisely God's will, by admonition and warning, morally to lead believers to heavenly blessedness and by the grace of the Holy Spirit to prompt them willingly to persevere in faith and love. It is therefore completely mistaken to reason from the admonitions of Holy Scripture to the possibility of a total loss of grace. This conclusion is illegitimate as when,

---

17. For further discussion of the many issues raised by this text, see Thomas R. Schreiner and Ardel B. Caneday, *The Race Set Before Us: A Biblical Theology of Perseverance and Assurance* (Downers Grove and Leicester: IVP, 2001); Thomas R. Schreiner, *Run to Win the Prize: Perseverance in the New Testament* (Nottingham: IVP, 2009).

in the case of Christ, people infer from his temptation that he was able
to sin. The certainty of the outcome does not render the means
superfluous but is inseparably connected with them in the decree of
God. Paul knew with certainty that in the case of shipwreck no one
would lose one's life, yet he declares, 'Unless these men stay in the ship,
you cannot be saved.' (Acts 27:22, 31).'[18]

© Thomas R. Schreiner, 2012

---

18. Herman Bavinck, *Reformed Dogmatics*, ed. John Bolt, tr. John Vriend,
     4 vols. (Grand Rapids: Baker, 2008), vol. 4, pp. 267–268.

6. ACCESS AND ARRIVAL

METAPHORS OF MOVEMENT TO MOTIVATE

Peter Walker

Hebrews is a motivational sermon, marked by urgency, passion and energy.[1] It is full of dynamic motion, urging us to not to sit still but to keep on the move. To achieve this effect the author develops a wide range of metaphors: we are to 'strive', to 'draw near', to 'go on to maturity'; we are not to 'fall away', 'be sluggish' or 'shrink back'; instead we are to 'draw near', to 'encourage one another' and to 'run'.[2]

Here we will focus on the two broad metaphors of movement which are predominant in Hebrews (those of 'approaching' and 'journeying on'). We will note the paradoxical interplay between them, and how this may help us understand the theme of assurance within the Christian life. We will also draw out some significant

---

1. On reading Hebrews as effectively an 'exhortatory sermon' or 'sermon-treatise', see e.g. D. A. Hagner, *Hebrews* (Peabody: Hendrickson, 1983) and W. L. Lane, *Hebrews: A Call to Commitment* (Peabody: Hendrickson, 1985).
2. These metaphors are found respectively in Heb. 4:11, 16; 6:1, 6, 12; 10:39; 10:22, 25; 12:1.

implications, not only for contemporary preaching, but also for how we should understand three important physical aspects of Old Testament faith (the temple, Jerusalem and the land) in the era of the new covenant.

A sermon: 'keep going'

Any reader of Hebrews cannot help but be aware that the author wants us to go on a journey and to keep going until we arrive. He wants to encourage perseverance, to warn against giving up in the Christian race, and to take people forward toward their final destination. A brief overview of some of the key language employed, especially in the exhortatory sections of the letter, will illustrate this point:

- We are not to *drift away* (2:1) from the message which we have heard, through 'neglecting such a great salvation'.
- Christian believers 'share in a heavenly calling' (3:1); in other words we have been given a heavenly destination, and therefore something to aim for.
- Unlike the Israelites who proved faithless in their desert wanderings and so did not enter God's rest, we must not develop an 'unbelieving heart' and thus '*fall away* from the living God' (3:12). There is indeed still a divine 'rest': 'Let us therefore strive to *enter* [*eiselthein*] that rest' (4:11).
- Knowing that we have a sympathetic high priest in Jesus, we are to '*draw near* [*proserchōmetha*] to the throne of grace' (4:16).
- Now that Jesus by his death and exaltation has 'entered' (*eisēlthen*) God's presence on our behalf (9:11–12, 24–25), we too can now have confidence to *approach* or *draw near* to the holy places by the blood of Jesus; we can '*draw near* [*proserchōmetha*] with a true heart in full assurance of faith' (10:22).
- We are not to throw away our confidence, but to '*endure*' (10:35–36), knowing that we have a future great 'reward'; we are to live by faith and not '*shrink back*' (10:39).

- By faith we are to be convinced about divine realities which
  are still future ('hoped for') or invisible ('not seen') (11:1), like
  Abraham who '*went out* not knowing where he was *going*' and
  who 'was *looking forward* to the city that has foundations'
  (11:8–10).
- We are to '*run* with endurance the race that is set before us,
  looking to Jesus . . . who for the joy that was set before him
  endured the cross' (12:1–2). The Jesus whom we follow is
  himself a 'pioneer' (12:2, NRSV), has run and completed this
  race, and is now '*seated*' at God's 'right hand'. So we should
  not '*become weary or faint-hearted*' (12:3), but instead 'lift your
  drooping hands and strengthen your weak knees, and make
  straight paths for your feet' (12:12–13).
- Moreover, instead of fearful Mount Sinai, our destination
  is a glorious one, Mount Zion, the heavenly Jerusalem, to
  which, paradoxically, we have already *arrived* (note the
  perfect tense [*proselēlythate*] in 12:22: 'you *have* come').
- Finally we are not to be '*led away* by diverse . . . teachings'
  (13:9). Mindful of Jesus' short but momentous journey
  from the city of Jerusalem to Golgotha, we are to '*go to
  him* outside the camp and bear the reproach he endured';
  we are to set our hope on the 'city that is to come'
  (13:13–14).

The author is evidently using a wide variety of what might be called
'metaphors of movement', prompting and provoking his readers to
keep going on the road.

In this process we can note in passing how he uses a masterful
blend of encouragement and challenge. As summarized in the table
below, this first-century 'sermon in writing' has evidently been con-
structed with consummate care. Aware that his audience may contain
people on a sliding scale of negativity (that is, from those who are
merely feeling discouraged to those who are tempted to abandon
the faith), he carefully alternates his tone: at one moment, severely
warning and chiding those tempted in the latter direction, at another,

gently encouraging those tempted in the former direction. There
are important lessons here for modern preachers.[3]

The preacher's pastoral balance in Hebrews

Words of comfort	Words of challenge
1:1–14	2:1–4
2:5–18	3:1 – 4:13
4:14 – 5:10	5:11 – 6:8
6:9 – 10:25	10:25–31
10:32 – 11:40	12:1–21
12:22–24	12:25–29
13:1–8	13:9–14
13:15–25	

More importantly, however, we should observe how underneath
this wide array of images there are two predominant metaphors which
stand out. The first image (used in chs. 4 – 5 and 11 – 12) summarizes
his basic message: that faith in Jesus has placed us on a journey; we
must not fall aside from that journey but instead keep pressing towards
the goal of eventual arrival. This could be termed the metaphor of
'journeying' or 'pilgrimage'; believers are travelling towards an
important destination. Yet, sandwiched in the centre of that image
(chs. 5 – 10), the author uses a second metaphor to assure us that we
have immediate access to the Holy of Holies. This could be termed
the metaphor of 'approach' or 'cultic access'; even now believers can
enjoy God's presence and have access to his throne of grace.

Noting these two predominant images, it is appropriate to speak
of believers being portrayed in Hebrews as 'cultic pilgrims'.[4] This

---

3. See further below.
4. See e.g. W. G. Johnsson, 'The Pilgrimage: A Motif in the Book of
   Hebrews', *JBL* 97 (1978), pp. 239–251, who also speaks of believers
   being a 'cultic community on the move' (p. 249). The classic work
   on the 'pilgrimage' theme in Hebrews remains E. Käsemann, *The
   Wandering People of God*, tr. Roy A. Harrisville and Irving Sandberg
   (Minneapolis: Augsburg, 1984).

is not an especially attractive phrase, but it encapsulates well the
biblical background to these two metaphors: on the one hand,
the act of pilgrimage up to Jerusalem; on the other, the temple cult
(which continued the worship of the 'tabernacle', as referred to in
Hebrews). Both these Old Testament motifs have been taken over
by the author and, as we shall see, are now given a whole new
meaning in the light of Christ's coming. Yet first, we should note
just how much of the rhetorical force of Hebrews' argument as a
sermon depends on these two images and, crucially, on the paradoxical interplay between them.

A paradox

In the first image we are still pilgrims and have not yet arrived; in
the second we are already at our destination. In the first we do not
yet enjoy an intimate access to God's presence, in the second we
assuredly do. Each image makes sense on its own, but we cannot
easily understand how they can be true at the same time.

At this point, however, we realize that the author of Hebrews
has put into picture form the biblical paradox which is often referred
to elsewhere as the 'now but not yet' tension within the New
Testament. We already have come to fullness of life in Christ, but
we still need to be filled with the Spirit (Col. 2:10; Eph. 5:18). We
have a new identity in Christ, but we still often do not live according
to it (Rom. 6 – 7). We are already 'glorified', but in our experience
we are not (Rom. 8:30); we are fully forgiven, but still need to confess
our on-going sins (1 John 1:8–9); we are already 'seated' with Christ
in heaven, but we still need to keep 'standing' in our earthly battles
(Eph. 2:6; 6:11). In some senses we already are in heaven, in other
senses we clearly are not.

At this point the author reveals consummate pastoral skill. He
knows that one of the best ways to motivate people to keep going
on to the end of the road is not only to allure them with images of
what it will be like to have crossed the finishing-line, but actually to

teach them that they have already arrived! That is why in chapter 12, when his readers are still clearly running the race, he can quite deliberately state that they have *already* arrived in the heavenly Jerusalem: 'you have come to Mount Zion' (12:22). The temple imagery serves the same function. Thus, at the end of chapter 4, we can even now 'draw near' the throne of grace and find help in our present need; and in chapter 10 we can draw near with full assurance of faith. Right now, even in the middle of our journey, we can enjoy intimate access to God. The temple imagery is thus brilliantly placed in the central chapters of the book, close to its heart, acting thereby as an incredible incentive for the readers to keep going. Faith again, is the 'assurance of things hoped for, the conviction of things not seen' (11:1).

Modern preachers would do well to note this strategy. Preaching legalistic duty seldom motivates. By contrast, preaching God's grace and all that God has done for us, unlocks a deep response of gratitude. When a vision is cast of who we truly are in Christ, it creates in us the desire to be now in practice what we already truly are in spiritual reality. We want, as it were, to pour ourselves into the marvellous mould that God has already created for us. And when preachers speak with faith-filled vision of heavenly reality as it now is, that spurs us on to make that a reality now on earth. Biblical preaching will always have this dynamic of not merely describing the problems of our present experience, but also deliberately pointing towards the spiritual, heavenly realities, which, even though invisible to us, are fundamentally true in this present moment and which one day will be manifested.

Finally on this point, let's notice how awareness of these two paradoxical images in Hebrews may help us in dealing with the paradoxes surrounding the Christian doctrine of assurance. One of the key points at issue in the Reformation was a rediscovery of the New Testament's teaching on this vital issue: believers in Christ can have a 'full assurance of faith' (Heb. 10:22), and know that they are already forgiven and justified in God's sight, with no fear of eventual judgment (Rom. 8:1, etc.); the believer has passed over 'from death to life' (John 5:24). This has ever since been a hallmark of evangelical teaching. In the Reformation period this stood in marked contrast to a religious system which was characterized by a host of doubts and uncertainties and which would view such claims to Christian assurance as conceited, arrogant and potentially disastrous from an ethical and pastoral perspective ('surely telling people they are totally forgiven will only encourage them to sin now with gleeful abandon'). To this day this doctrine of assurance is susceptible to the same types of critique and scepticism. In such circles one is therefore far more likely to be told that the Christian life is like setting out on a journey – but most definitely not a journey in which you have somehow already arrived at your destination the very moment you begin!

Yet Hebrews does precisely that. Yes, the Christian life is a journey, but, yes, we have already arrived. By using the imagery of the journey, the author to some degree takes the sting out of the accusation that one is falsely encouraging an arrogant sense of arrival. Yet, by complementing this with the imagery from the temple, he simultaneously prevents this journey from being marked by the kind of doubt and uncertainty that would eventually cripple the traveller altogether.

And this may then help us to understand how it is that the book of Hebrews, despite teaching so clearly this doctrine of assurance, is at the same time the book which has the two most fearful passages in the New Testament warning believers about potential apostasy (6:4–6; 10:26–31). The writer can speak of people coming to 'taste the heavenly gift', yet warn that they may so 'spurn the Son of God' that they eventually experience God's judgment. At first sight one might think the author accepts that a genuine believer might eventually not experience salvation, but judgment – the very opposite of what the doctrine of assurance would seem to suggest.

This issue is helpfully discussed in more detail in Tom Schreiner's chapter in this volume. Here we need simply highlight the point that this apparent tension within the argument of Hebrews is all part of this much larger conceptual world that the author has painted.

Within the image of the journey, these warning passages sit quite comfortably, as exhortations not to go backwards but to go forwards. Within the world of the image of cultic approach, they sit less comfortably. Modern preachers will need to pray for wisdom to discern the nature of their audience: are these people who need warning and challenge (perhaps precisely to sort out the genuine believers from those who are not), or are they people who, though genuine believers, have become discouraged and fearful, and who need the ministry of assurance and encouragement?

Temple, city and land: 'leave behind'

So as readers of Hebrews we are to see ourselves as 'cultic pilgrims' – those who simultaneously have access into God's presence right now, yet are also on a journey towards that final goal. Within the cultic imagery we have arrived, but within the pilgrim imagery we have not. However, we must now ask: what are the biblical-theological implications of the author's use of these Old Testament metaphors? Should believers be developing new attitudes towards the temple and Jerusalem in the light of Christ's coming?

However, some may still be questioning whether 'pilgrim' is quite the right word. After all, this term is not expressly used in Hebrews, where the believer's journey is likened instead either to the Israelites' wandering in the desert (chs. 3 – 4) or to an athletics race (ch. 12). Yet this is to forget that in the Old Testament pilgrimage is encouraged as a religious practice, and the goal of such pilgrimage is Jerusalem. When we note that the ultimate destination of the journey in Hebrews is 'Mount Zion . . . the heavenly Jerusalem' (12:22), it becomes clear that the author has indeed appropriated this biblical category of pilgrimage and reapplied it for his audience in a new way. Moreover, in the light of the way many of the traditions associated with Sinai had been transposed by Old Testament writers onto Mount Zion (as seen, for example, in Ps. 68), it is not unreasonable to suppose that the pilgrimage to Zion practised in the Old Testament period was itself seen as in some way replicating or repeating the Israelites' original journey through the desert towards the goal of the Promised Land. If so, then the author's earlier use of the Israelites' wanderings may also legitimately be seen as part of this 'pilgrimage' motif. After all, if pilgrimage is a way of referring to a journey inspired by faith towards a divinely appointed destination, then that is a very good description of all the journeying described by the author of Hebrews.

The important point to note is that the author has taken up these various Old Testament journeys (whether to the Promised Land or to Jerusalem, the city of God) and has given them a whole new meaning in the light of Christ. Biblical 'pilgrimage' is now being substantially recast: as a foreshadowing of the journey on which all Christian believers are called to embark – the journey towards the heavenly Jerusalem.

Modern preachers need to note carefully the important biblical-theological moves being made here by the author of Hebrews. There is, as I have argued more fully elsewhere, a wholesale re-evaluation in Hebrews of each of the three great physical realities which had become central within Old Testament faith and practice: temple, city and land.[5] It is readily noted that his second image (the 'cultic' one) is used by the author to wean his readers away from a focus on the Jerusalem temple. What is not so often noticed is that his first image (the 'pilgrim' one) is intended to have the same effect with regard to the city and the land. Although devotion to the city and the land may not have been so strong a temptation for his readers when compared to the temple, the author is putting down some clear markers that any previous focus on the land or upon Jerusalem is now out of place for Jesus-focused believers. Now that Christ has introduced the era of the new covenant, these three aspects of Old Testament faith are all, in some senses, to be left behind.

---

5. Each of these three themes in Hebrews is analyzed in detail in my *Jesus and the Holy City: New Testament Perspectives on Jerusalem* (Grand Rapids: Eerdmans, 1986), ch. 6.

The temple

It is worth noting, then, how the author argues his case with each
of these three realities. Concerning the temple, his central chapters
prove to be a powerful argument for its effective redundancy in the
light of Christ. Although the Old Testament pattern of worship had
been clearly instituted by God (the Jerusalem temple was modelled
upon the instructions given by God to Moses for the original 'tabernacle' in the wilderness), it could now be seen to have been but a
foreshadowing of the ultimate reality found through Christ. Jesus
through his death has offered the one sacrifice for sin and has gone
into God's immediate presence in the true Holy of Holies, the
heavenly tabernacle, of which the Jerusalem temple was but an
earthly counterpart (or 'anti-type', 9:24). Seen in the light of Christ,
we can now detect that there were certain inherent weaknesses in
the previous system: how could the blood of animals truly remove
sin?, and was not the annual Day of Atonement more an 'annual
reminder of sins' rather than an assurance that their sins had already
been fully forgiven (10:1–4; 9:9)? Now, however, through Christ the
reality has come, revealing the previous pattern as a mere 'copy and
shadow' (8:5).

As a result, Jewish believers in Jesus must abandon their loyalty or
sense of affinity with the Jerusalem temple. It cannot offer them what
they now have through Jesus – full assurance of sins forgiven. In his
concluding exhortation the author effectively presents them with a
clear choice: through Jesus' sacrificial death for sins 'we have an altar
[a means of being forgiven] from which those who serve the tent
[those priests serving the temple cult in Jerusalem] have no right to
eat' (13:10). There are now two mutually exclusive systems. Those
who are focused on the Jerusalem temple cannot enjoy what we now
have through Jesus, and those who receive their forgiveness through
Jesus have no need of the Jerusalem temple. We must make our
choice. And, to press this choice home upon his readers, the author
paints a graphic picture of Jesus going out from Jerusalem towards
Golgotha, being cast out of the 'camp' just as the scapegoat victim
was cast out from the temple: 'So Jesus also suffered outside the gate

in order to sanctify the people through his own blood. Therefore let us go out to him outside the camp . . . ' (13:12–13). In effect he is saying, 'Choose Jesus; receive the sacrifice for your sins offered by him, and do not go hankering back to the temple's sacrificial system.'

It remains a matter of conjecture in what precise way the original readers of Hebrews were being tempted by the attractions of the temple system.[6] Whatever the actual context, however, the author's line of argument is plain: the Jerusalem temple is no longer to be a source of spiritual nurture. Moreover, this means that the temple is now effectively redundant. As argued elsewhere, the enigmatic phrases in 8:13 (where the trappings of the first covenant are described as 'obsolete' and 'growing old' and as 'ready to vanish away', translated by some as 'close to destruction') might well be the author's subtle hint that, though the Jerusalem temple continues outwardly to function, its days are numbered. As the building which encapsulates the old order and which has now been rendered obsolete through the manifestation of the new covenant, it no longer has any divine purpose. It is indeed 'close to destruction'. If writing in the early 60s AD, the author may thus here be taking on the role of a prophet; as Jesus had already warned, there would soon come a time when the temple would be destroyed (Mark 13:2, etc.).[7]

---

6. Lindars' suggestion has much to commend it. Citing the evidence of Josephus (*Antiquities* 14.213–216), he argues that the readers of Hebrews were being invited by their friends to attend 'communal dinners which were held on Jewish feast days in Diaspora Judaism'. 'These were one way in which Jews far away from Jerusalem maintained the sense of solidarity with the temple and its cultus.' This was a 'resumption of Jewish practises which expressed solidarity with the covenant people and with the Temple at its heart . . . ' (B. Lindars, 'The Rhetorical Structure of Hebrews', *NTS* 35 [1989], pp. 388, 404). Cf. also W. L. Lane, *Hebrews 9–13*, WBC 47B (Dallas: Word, 1991), pp. 530–536.

7. For the arguments for a pre-70 date for Hebrews, see my *Jesus and the Holy City*, pp. 227–234. This is the majority view of most commentaries. For a post-70 date, however, see e.g. M. E. Isaacs, *Sacred Space*, JSNTSS 7 (Sheffield: JSOT, 1992), pp. 44, 67, and H. Koester, *Introduction to the New Testament*, vol. 2 (Philadelphia: Fortress, 1982), p. 272.

This theme of the temple's redundancy is readily noticed by modern readers; and Christian theology has made much of the way Jesus' death replaces the need for the temple. What may not so readily be noticed is how active a temptation this was for the original readers and also how prophetic and courageous were the author's words – written *before* the temple's destruction, not after it.

We should also note that the author has been similarly courageous in offering a critique of the two other important realities which may have been pulling at the Jewish hearts of his hearers: their mother-city of Jerusalem and their land. Even if the original audience was located in Rome and far away from the land of Israel, first-century history blatantly reveals that strong passions could be aroused in Jewish hearts in the cause of defending their city and their land from pagan domination. Throughout Jesus' ministry the tension in Palestine was palpable, and by the 60s, prior to the First Jewish Revolt, the tensions in Jerusalem were reaching fever-pitch. In this tumultuous season, it would not be surprising if, even in the diaspora, Jewish loyalties were being raised on behalf of the nationalist cause. And the response of Jewish-Christians (such as the original audience of Hebrews) would have been closely watched. Into this delicate situation the author of Hebrews offers a subtle but carefully worded critique of all this passionate focus on the land and the city.

The land of Israel

Concerning the land he makes it clear the Promised Land was only ever a divine gift for those who were faithful and obedient; Israel's God had evidently withdrawn this gift from the original Israelite generation, so presumably he might be prepared to do the same in this present season. More explicitly, the author uses the category of 'rest' (from Ps. 95) to signal that the gift of the Promised Land was always a pointer to something greater, namely, God's gift of 'Sabbath-rest' and blessing for his people. This, the author argues, is precisely what is available now to Christian believers in the first century; and indeed, it was also that which was never properly given even in the days of Joshua: 'For if Joshua had given them rest, God would not have spoken of another day later on. So then, there remains a Sabbath rest for the people of God' (4:8–9). The author's argument is slightly condensed here, but his main point is clear: his readers' focus should not be on the physical Promised Land (which had its ambiguities even at the time) but rather on what it always signified – God's promised 'rest'.

Exactly the same argument is developed again in chapter 11. The author explicitly refers to the 'land of promise' (11:9) in his portrait of Abraham, but he immediately highlights how the patriarchs did not settle there but viewed it as a foreign land. Instead they were 'looking forward to the city that has foundations' (11:10). A few verses later, he makes the same point: the patriarchs considered themselves 'strangers and exiles'; in speaking thus they were evidently 'seeking a homeland', but not the one 'from which they had gone out', but a 'better country, that is, a heavenly one'.

The author now at last explicitly opens up the concept of a 'heavenly' country or land, thereby showing that this has been in his mind all along. The Promised Land in Palestine was not the end-game, either for the Israelites in Numbers or for the Patriarchs in Genesis. The physical land was always a pointer to a deeper reality, a heavenly one. So, although he does not expressly use the terminology here as he does of the temple, presumably he would have seen the Promised Land as a 'shadow', a physical reality which was designed by God to point upwards and forwards to an ultimate spiritual reality. If so, the author contends, this is what his audience should be focused on. If any of them finds themselves tempted to put their emotional or political energies into the current arguments and fighting over the land, they are focusing in the wrong direction. Through Christ they always have a secure promise of a Sabbath-rest, and they should be giving their greatest attention to ensuring that they do not miss out on that through unbelief.

Jerusalem

This same pattern is seen, finally, with regard to Jerusalem. In biblical thought this central city within the life of God's people was understood to be a 'holy city', specially selected by God: 'the Lord loves the gates of Zion more than all the dwelling places of Jacob' (Ps. 87:2). Much of this status was bound up with the temple within the city, which in a more particular sense was the dwelling place of the Name, the place where God's *shekinah* glory had dwelt for a season before the departure of that glory in the exile (Ezek. 11:23). Yet there was a sense in which the wider, inhabited city was also a place where God was present amongst his people, so Jerusalem could be termed the 'City of God' (Ps. 87). Jesus himself picks up the terminology of Psalm 48 in referring to it as the 'city of the great King' (Matt. 5:35; Ps. 48:1).

Yet in recent history Jesus himself had also wept over the city and had challenged its religious leaders (Luke 19:41–44). Most obviously he had dramatically cleansed the temple in a prophetic act symbolizing that, like the barren fig tree, it was ripe for judgment and destruction (Mark 11:12–21). Yet his words of judgment were not confined to the temple but spread out to encompass the city as a whole: 'O Jerusalem, Jerusalem, the city that kills the prophets and stones those who are sent to it!' (Luke 13:34). Although Jesus had himself longed to place his protective arms around her, the time was coming when instead the city would be surrounded by Roman armies (Luke 19:43). All this would come about because the city 'did not know the time of your visitation' (Luke 19:44), the time when God came to her in the person of Jesus.

So, some thirty years before the writing of Hebrews, Jesus himself had signalled a painful and dramatic shift in God's purposes towards this former holy city. The fact that this city had then rejected her Messiah and been the scene of his crucifixion would only have confirmed this negative judgment upon the city. The author of Hebrews now articulates this shift. We have already seen how in chapter 11 he twice introduces the concept of a 'heavenly city' as the true object of the patriarchs' desires when sojourning in the

Promised Land (11:14, 16). This neatly prepares the reader for the great climax in chapter 12, where the goal of their journeying is 'Mount Zion . . . the heavenly Jerusalem'. Evidently the author wants his readers' attention to be focused not on the earthly city but on the heavenly one.

Yet, just in case we might think this reference to the heavenly Jerusalem is merely a rhetorical flourish (a colourfully up-beat ending to his message), the author pointedly returns to the theme of Jerusalem in chapter 13. In this more down-to-earth context, the negative corollary (that the earthly Jerusalem is not to be the object of our loyalty) comes more clearly to the fore. He expressly asks his readers to remember that recent brute historical reality, when the earthly Jerusalem rejected Jesus and, as it were, cast him from her midst: 'Jesus suffered outside the gate'. Then he continues with an appeal that, if we are truly followers of Jesus, we should now follow him 'outside the camp', as it were, turning our own backs on Jerusalem. And his final reason is instructive: 'for here we have no lasting city, but we seek the city that is to come' (13:14). The physical city of Jerusalem is not a city that will 'last'; if we invest it with our aspirations, it will let us down. Our focus instead should be on the heavenly city 'that is to come'.

The author's argument is deftly made and couched in quite enigmatic and evocative language. This means that we do not receive an outright and blatant attack on either the temple or the city. This was his last crucial appeal to the hearts of his audience, and the appeal needed to be made with great care and sensitivity. Yet, if there were any amongst his readers who were focusing for whatever reason (political, national, spiritual, personal) on either the temple's sacrificial system or on the nation's capital, Jerusalem, then the author's alternative counsel and advice was abundantly clear: 'don't go there!' Instead, 'let us go to Jesus' (13:13).

Interpretive tools

Today's preachers would do well to note these big transitions made by the author of Hebrews. This re-evaluation of the Old Testament's central geographical *realia* can indeed be found scattered throughout the pages of the New Testament; yet they are perhaps concentrated upon most fully here in Hebrews. Here, in this vital and often over-looked book, we are given key tools of biblical interpretation. Many passages on which we will be called to preach will make some passing reference to the temple, Jerusalem or the land and we will need, even if briefly, to help our congregations to know how to understand these things in the light of the new covenant. For example, we may need to say 'the Psalmist in our passage speaks of his desire to find's God's presence in the temple, but today we can apply this to our desire to experience more of God's presence as found in Jesus and his Spirit'. These kinds of 'biblical-theological moves' are necessary in all good biblical preaching, but we will only make them if we have confidence in the shape of our own biblical theology – and know that it is indeed derived from the Bible. The book of Hebrews here can become a vital bedrock and foundation to give us that confidence.

There may be some of us who see issues concerning the temple, city and land as rather remote and irrelevant. Others may see the relevance of showing Christ's fulfilment of the temple theme, but then question whether many in our congregations are much bothered about Jerusalem and the land of Israel. Yet issues to do with Zion and Israel are notoriously divisive within the modern church. Some pastors relate how this is the one topic which they dread referring to in their preaching for fear of the backlash they may receive or of the church split that might result. And, if this is true in the West, how much more so is this true in the contemporary Middle East. I was recently preaching in an evangelical church in a major Arabic-speaking city, where the pastor explained how much opprobrium his church members experience (from the government, the majority Muslim population and the historic churches) because, as Bible-believing evangelical Christians, it is immediately presumed that they must be embracing a theology which straightforwardly backs the State of Israel. Many church congregations in the Middle East therefore avoid using the Psalms in their worship and will only rarely preach from the Old Testament. Three-quarters of the Bible is not being used because the church leaders and preachers do not have confidence in their own biblical theology. How much is the book of Hebrews needed!

Preaching Hebrew's message: 'go out to him'

Finally, however, we need to consider how contemporary preachers might apply the focus of Hebrews' appeal in contexts where temple, city and land are not live issues for their congregation. At this point the preacher needs, as it were, to *go back up one level* (to use an image from our modern computer filing systems). At this level we can see that the author's main purpose is to ensure a continued faithfulness to Jesus, because he is unique and better than anything else upon which we might lean.[8] So we need to be looking out for those things

8. This more general purpose may indicate that Hebrews is being written, not just when the issues of the temple are becoming critical for diaspora Judaism, but also when the Christian community is facing the threat of persecution for not being in the eyes of the Roman authorities a 'permitted religion' *(religio licita)* as was Judaism. Elsewhere, in my *In the Steps of Saint Paul* (Oxford: LionHudson, 2008) I have raised the possibility that Hebrews, even if evidently not written by Paul himself, might perhaps have effectively been *commissioned* by him. After his arrival in Rome (in March 60) Paul may have become acutely aware of the rising threat of persecution in Nero's Rome – as the imperial authorities began to sense that the Christian faith could no longer be seen merely as a variant within Judaism. Gentile believers would be particularly vulnerable; and Jewish believers would be strongly tempted to hide under the safe 'umbrella' of non-Christian Judaism, perhaps returning exclusively to within the synagogue. In these circumstances any pleading by the apostle Paul himself would have been useless: after all, he was the self-styled 'apostle to the Gentiles' whose trial in Rome would only reveal the worldwide and Gentile nature of the Christian faith. So Paul might well have recognized the need to encourage an absent but trusted Jewish leader of the Roman church to write to them. We cannot now determine who that was, but this particular reconstruction serves to strengthen the suggestion that people such as Aquila and Priscilla were among those to whom Paul might have turned.

– both in ourselves and in our congregations – which become false grounds of confidence, or spiritual cul-de-sacs. In the imagery of Hebrews 12:2, we need to be working out what are the 'weights' and 'sins' which are holding us back. And we need to be encouraging people to lay these things aside, to keep their eyes fixed on Jesus and to 'run the race'.

Put another way, as in his graphic exhortation in the final chapter, we are to 'go out' to Jesus, going 'outside the camp' and bearing 'the reproach he bore' (13:13). Some of the things we are called to 'lay aside' are things which give us respectability and we need, if need be, to accept 'disgrace' in our following of Jesus. Some of them instead may be things long treasured (as Jerusalem perhaps had been for the original readers), but we must hold them with a lightness of touch. Finding the precise application will require the pastor to be much in prayer and also to love the congregation deeply.

And the appeal will then need to be made with all the pastoral skill so evident in Hebrews. We will need to exhibit the incredible balance found in this sermon (as noted in the table, p. 110) between challenge and encouragement; there will need to be crystal clarity and pointed argument, but also incredible gentleness and sensitivity. The word of God 'pierces' our inmost being (4:12) and we will need to preach that word aware of its cutting power. Yet we must also present to our congregations the overwhelming 'sympathy' and understanding that is found in Jesus our great High Priest (4:15). As the author reminds his readers just before making that final exhortation: 'Jesus Christ is the same, yesterday, today and forever' (13:8). Giving our congregations a vision of the unchanging faithfulness of Jesus will then enable them to hear any challenges as coming not from us but from this merciful 'shepherd of the sheep' (13:20). And those sheep, when they hear the Master's voice, will respond to his gracious call.

© Peter Walker, 2012

7. PERFECTION

ACHIEVED AND EXPERIENCED

David G. Peterson

The perfecting of Christ is mentioned three times in Hebrews (2:10; 5:9; 7:28). Four times the inability of the law to perfect believers is argued (7:11, 19; 9:9; 10:1), and three times the perfection found in Christ is affirmed (10:14; 11:40; 12:23). Using related terminology, the writer also urges his readers to maturity (5:11 – 6:2) and points them to Christ as the perfecter of faith (12:2). Given the spread of these references and their role in the development of the argument, a brief survey of their meaning and inter-relationship will expose the importance of this theme for a proper understanding of Hebrews.

Some methodological issues

Various interpretations have been offered to explain the concept of perfection in Hebrews, related to different assessments of the background and purpose of this document. The elastic adaptability of *teleios* and its derivatives in biblical and extra-biblical usage encourages interpreters to suggest the relevance of some associations and to reject others, according to their suppositions about the religious context in which the document was written. DeSilva rightly observes that 'the semantic range of this word group is indeed broad, so much so that the audience of Hebrews would itself need careful clues from the author to understand what any word from this group connotes in a particular setting.'[1]

So, for example, perfection has been understood in Gnostic terms to mean glorification. Some scholars have argued that Hebrews was influenced by the mystery religions to present Christian worship as the true way to participate in the cult of heaven, with Jesus as high priest. Noting a Septuagintal use of the terminology in certain cultic contexts, others have argued that it describes a 'priestly' consecration to God. Observing the use of parallel terms in the Qumran literature, others have taken the terminology to refer to moral and spiritual transformation.[2]

The influence of Greco-Roman culture on Hebrews is evident in its 'elegant language and elevated rhetoric', but the extent to which it may have influenced the *argument* is still much debated.[3] Certain affinities with the letters of Paul, Stephen's speech in Acts 7 and 1 Peter show that Hebrews is much more obviously located 'within the mainstream of early Christian tradition'.[4] Against the view that

---

1. D. A. deSilva, *Perseverance in Gratitude: A Socio-Rhetorical Commentary on the Epistle 'to the Hebrews'* (Grand Rapids: Eerdmans, 2000), p. 195. Cf. P. J. Du Plessis, *TELEIOS: The Idea of Perfection in the New Testament* (Kampen: Kok, 1959), p. 212.

2. I have surveyed and critiqued a range of such approaches to the issue in *Hebrews and Perfection. An Examination of the Concept of Perfection in the 'Epistle to the Hebrews'*, SNTSMS 47 (Cambridge: Cambridge University Press, 1982; reprinted as a paperback 2005), pp. 1–20.

3. Cf. P. T. O'Brien, *The Letter to the Hebrews*, PNTC (Grand Rapids: Eerdmans, 2010), pp. 36–40.

4. O'Brien, *Hebrews*, p. 43. However, O'Brien (p. 40), is aware that various aspects of Hellenistic and Palestinian culture and religion could have influenced the thinking of the writer through the mainstream of early Christian tradition.

Hebrews was written to Gentile Christians in danger of retreating
to some form of Hellenistic syncretism, it is much more likely that
it was written to a predominantly Jewish Christian group in danger
of returning to a reliance on the cultic structures of the Mosaic
covenant.[5]

Linguistically, it is important to note several things. First, the verb
teleioun is used more extensively in Hebrews than any other member
of this word group (2:10; 5:9; 7:19, 28; 9:9; 10:1, 14; 11:40; 12:23).
Formally, it means 'to make *teleios*', and so 'to make complete' or 'to
perfect', and it is widely used in ancient Greek literature with a range
of applications. The verb itself carries no material associations of
a moral or technical kind, and distinct content can only be given by
the context on each occasion.[6]

Secondly, the use of this verb in an essentially non-moral sense,
to refer to the perfecting of someone in a particular vocation, is of
special interest for the study of Hebrews.[7] In such contexts, the
completion of a task or the occurrence of some significant event
brings about the perfecting of someone in a role or calling.

Thirdly, some have argued that the particular LXX use of *teleioun
tas cheiras* (lit. 'to perfect the hands'), with reference to the consecration of Levitical priests (Exod. 29:9, 29, 33, 35; Lev. 8:33; 16:32; Num.
3:3), suggests a cultic application of this verb in Hebrews. However,
this strange LXX rendering of a technical Hebrew expression must
be understood as a syntactical unit. When the translators use *teleioun,*
instead of more literal alternatives, they appear to imply that the
high point of the consecration ceremony was to 'perfect' or 'qualify'
the hands for priestly sacrifice and thus to 'perfect' or 'qualify' the
priest for his role. The verb is being used in a purely formal way in
these passages. It is not legitimate to argue that *teleioun* apart from

5. Cf. S. D. Mackie, *Eschatology and Exhortation in the Epistle to the Hebrews,*
WUNT II.223 (Tübingen: Mohr Siebeck, 2007), pp. 10–17; O'Brien,
Hebrews, pp. 9–13.

6. Peterson, *Hebrews and Perfection,* pp. 21–23. Cf. H. W. Attridge, *The Epistle
to the Hebrews,* Hermeneia (Philadelphia: Fortress, 1989), pp. 83–87.

7. E.g. Herodotus III.86; Sophocles, *Electra* 1508–10; Luke 13:32.

tas cheiras acquires special cultic significance and that the writer of Hebrews could use it to mean 'consecrate (as a priest)'.[8]

Fourthly, although Philo and early Christian writers employ *teleioun* in conjunction with their respective soteriologies, it cannot simply be assumed that the word carries similar associations in Hebrews. The writer's usage must be examined with reference to his own theological emphases and the views that he challenges. Only the context in each case and the object of the verb in particular can indicate the sense of each application.

The perfecting of Christ

The broad perspective
The first reference to the perfecting of Christ comes in a passage where eschatology, Christology and soteriology are interwoven in a concise and profound way. The theme of Christ's eschatological rule, in which angels are merely 'ministering spirits' (1:5–14), is resumed after the brief word of warning in 2:1–4. However, the new perspective in 2:5–9 is that Jesus assumes this rule by fulfilling Psalm 8:4–6, being made 'for a little while lower than the angels', but then 'crowned with glory and honour because of the suffering of death, so that by the grace of God he might taste death for everyone'.[9]

Incarnation, death, heavenly exaltation and enthronement are the means by which the Messiah is glorified and begins his heavenly reign. But the final words of 2:9 indicate that, by the grace of God, his death is experienced 'for everyone' (*hyper pantos*). The writer goes

---

8. Cf. Peterson, *Hebrews and Perfection*, pp. 26–30, 71–73, against G. Delling, *TDNT*, vol. 8, pp. 79–84; W. L. Lane, *Hebrews*, WBC 47, 2 vols. (Dallas: Word, 1991), p. 57.

9. Ps. 8 seems to have been applied to Christ because the words 'putting everything in subjection under his feet' pick up the theme of absolute dominion from Ps. 110:1, which is cited in Heb. 1:13. Cf. 1 Cor. 15:25–27; Eph. 1:20–22; Phil. 3:21.

on to argue that Jesus' death makes atonement for sin, because he offers himself 'to bear the sins of many' (9:28), thereby making it possible for those who are called to share in his eternal inheritance (2:17; 9:27–28; 9:15).

The idea that Jesus is the man who fulfils Psalm 8 is developed in 2:10–16 to show how his achievement as 'pioneer' brings salvation to those who belong to him. A clear link with the preceding section is provided by the connective *gar* ('for'). God's action in Christ is described as 'fitting' for him, meaning consistent with his character and purpose. As the one 'for whom and by whom all things exist', God in his sovereignty is able to fulfil his purpose for humanity, which is described as 'bringing many sons to glory'.[10] This picks up the notion of being 'crowned with glory and honour' from 2:7, 9, and more precisely defines those who benefit from the experience of the Son. Citing various biblical texts, these 'many sons' are then further described as his 'brothers', 'the children God has given me' and 'the offspring of Abraham' (2:12–16).

Given God's great purpose and his gracious character, it was fitting that he should 'perfect the leader who saves them through sufferings' (2:10, my translation). Every word in this sequence is significant. Jesus is perfected as *ton archēgon tēs sōtērias autōn*, suggesting that a vocational understanding of the verb is intended here. Although the noun *archēgos* can mean 'originator', 'source' or 'author' (as in Acts 3:15), most commentators consider that the preceding participle (*agagonta*) points to the rendering 'leader' or 'pioneer' (as in Acts 5:31).[11] Jesus is led by God through sufferings to glory, so that he becomes the leader of his people on the way to salvation

---

10. O'Brien, *Hebrews*, p. 104, n. 113, discusses various ways in which the participial clause here has been understood to function grammatically and syntactically.

11. So NRSV, TNIV. P. G. Müller, *EDNT*, vol. 1, p. 163, who has researched the use of this noun extensively, gives the basic meaning as 'he who is first, who stays at the head, who leads' (emphasis removed). NIV ('author') and ESV ('founder') do not adequately capture the notion of leadership demanded by the context.

(cf. 6:20, *prodromos*, 'forerunner'). However, there are also sugges-
tions in the context that the term could mean that Jesus is the unique
source of salvation for others (cf. 5:9, *aitios sōtērias*). This is the way
2:9 concludes ('so that by the grace of God he might taste death for
everyone'), and the qualifier in 2:10 ('of their salvation') indicates
that he has done for them what they could not do for themselves
(cf. 2:14–15; 7:25; 9:28). So my translation ('the leader who saves
them through sufferings') seeks to bring out both emphases.

God qualified Jesus or fully equipped him for his role 'through
sufferings' (*dia pathēmatōn*). This expression is different from the one
in 2:9 (*dia to pathēma tou thanatou*), where 'the suffering which consisted
in death' is said to have been the *ground* of his exaltation (the preposition is used with the accusative). In 2:10, the plural noun has in
view the whole experience associated with and leading up to his
death (cf. 2:17–18; 5:7–9). The preposition with the genitive indicates
that he was perfected *through* this process: his sufferings were not
simply a prelude to his perfecting or the reason for it. The view that
the perfecting of Christ refers to his glorification alone is inadequate
because it does not take account of these syntactical observations.[12]
It also does not sufficiently recognize the way 2:14–18 develops the
argument and prepares for the expanded exposition of his high-
priestly ministry in 4:14 – 5:10. Jesus is qualified to become 'a
merciful and faithful high priest in the service of God' by a whole
sequence of events:

> his proving in suffering, his redemptive death to fulfil the divine
> requirements for the perfect expiation of sins and his exaltation to glory

---

12. J. M. Scholer, *Proleptic Priests: Priesthood in the Epistle to the Hebrews*,
    JSNTSS 49 (Sheffield: JSOT, 1991), pp. 197–199, equates the
    perfecting of Jesus with his entrance into the presence of God.
    DeSilva, *Perseverance in Gratitude*, pp. 197–199 similarly limits it to his
    exaltation after death, but he acknowledges that the path through
    which Jesus passed towards his heavenly destiny is seen by the author
    to fit him for the ministry he performs 'on the other side'. Cf.
    Peterson, *Hebrews and Perfection*, pp. 67–71.

and honour. Thus perfected or qualified, he not only provides his brothers with the promise of sharing in his glory, but also continues to provide them with the necessary help to persevere in their calling and reach their heavenly destination.[13]

Qualified for heavenly high priesthood

The second reference to the perfecting of Jesus occurs in 5:9. This comes at the climax of a section comparing the qualifications for high priesthood under the old covenant with Jesus' qualifications for eschatological and heavenly high priesthood (5:1–10). Before this, there is an exhortation to recognize that 'we have a great high priest who has passed through the heavens', and so to 'hold fast our confession' (4:14; cf. 3:1–6). Moreover, the readers are urged to remember that 'we do not have a high priest who is unable to sympathize with our weaknesses, but one who in every respect has been tempted as we are, yet without sin' (4:15). Consequently, they are urged to draw near with confidence to the throne of grace, to 'receive mercy and find grace to help in time of need' (4:16).

Since there are similar exhortations at the end of the central doctrinal section (10:19–23), it would appear that these, together with the associated calls to meet and exhort one another (3:12–14; 10:24–25), are the main pastoral challenges of Hebrews. Jesus' qualifications for his priestly ministry in 5:5–10 are the first stage of an extended argument supporting the claims and encouragements of 4:14–16 and 10:19–25. In particular, the assertion that the ascended Jesus is a sympathetic high priest because of his earthly testing is developed here (5:7–8; cf. 2:18).

There is a chiastic structure in 5:1–10. A general description of high priestly ministry is first given: these men were appointed on behalf of others 'to offer gifts and sacrifices for sin' (v. 1). A necessary quality for dealing with sinful people is then highlighted

---

13. Peterson, *Hebrews and Perfection*, p. 73. The specifically priestly dimension of the writer's Christology does not emerge until 2:17.

(vv. 2–3),[14] followed by the requirement of a divine calling (v. 4). In reverse order, the high priesthood of Jesus is then presented in terms of his divine calling (vv. 5–6), the experience that enables him to sympathize with those who are tested (vv. 7–8), and a general description of his saving role as 'a high priest after the order of Melchizedek' (vv. 9–10).

The writer claims that 'Christ did not exult himself to be made a high priest', but he was appointed by the one who addressed him as 'my Son' in Psalm 2:7 and as 'a priest for ever after the order of Melchizedek' in Psalm 110:4 (5:5–6). Two major Christological strands are drawn together here and the implications are considered in what follows. Although he was the Son of God, destined to reign eternally at God's right hand (1:5–13), he 'learned obedience through what he suffered' (5:8). The reason for this is explained in what follows: 'and being made perfect, he became the source of eternal salvation to all who obey him, being designated by God a high priest after the order of Melchizedek' (5:9–10).

Learning obedience through what he suffered is explained with special reference to the experience of Jesus in the Garden of Gethsemane (5:7; cf. Mark 14:36; Matt. 26:39; Luke 22:42). The expressions 'in the days of his flesh' and 'with loud cries and tears' could suggest a wider reference to testing in his ministry, but only the Gethsemane narratives offer a clear picture of Jesus threatened by death and seeking escape from it. The description of God as the one 'who was able to save him from death' indicates the content of Jesus' prayer ('remove this cup from me').[15] This was the supreme moment of testing for him, when he was tempted to swerve from

---

14. The verb *metriopathein* in 5:2 is mostly translated 'deal gently', but literally means 'restrain or moderate one's anger' (cf. Peterson, *Hebrews and Perfection*, p. 83). It is closely related to *sympathēsai* in 4:15 ('sympathize, empathize'), but is not identical.

15. Although some have suggested the influence of certain psalms and John 12:27–28 on the language of 5:7, this does not remove the need to link the verse with the Gethsemane traditions. Cf. Peterson, *Hebrews and Perfection*, pp. 86–89.

doing the will of his Father because of the suffering and alienation he anticipated.

The claim that he was 'heard because of his reverence' (*apo tēs eulabeias*) corresponds to the second part of Jesus' prayer in Gethsemane ('yet not what I will, but what you will'). When he brought his will into submission to the will of the Father, he expressed true piety or godliness. The answer to Jesus' prayer was salvation, 'not *from* temporal torment and death, but *in* and *through* such death'.[16] Positively, his prayer for salvation from death issued in the glory and victory of the cross and his triumphant resurrection.

When the writer goes on to describe the Son as 'being made perfect' (*teleiōtheis*), he implies that the learning of obedience through what he suffered was part of the process by which he was qualified to be 'the source of eternal salvation to all who obey him' (5:9). As in 2:10, a process is in view, and Jesus is perfected in his role as saviour of others. This is then related to his appointment by God as 'a high priest after the order of Melchizedek' (5:10), though the implications of this last claim are not really drawn out until Hebrews 7. The perfecting of Jesus as 'source of eternal salvation' involved his atoning death and his heavenly exaltation, so that as heavenly high priest, he could 'save to the uttermost those who draw near to God through him' (7:25). But it also involved the process leading up to his death.

There is no sense of educative correction in 5:7–8, as if Jesus had imperfections that needed to be overcome. We have already been told that he was 'in every respect . . . tempted as we are, yet without sin' (4:15), and the writer will soon affirm that he 'offered himself without blemish to God' (9:14). At one level, he had to suffer because he was called to fulfil the redemptive role of the Servant of the Lord,

---

16. R. E. Omark, 'The Saving of the Saviour: Exegesis and Christology in Hebrews 5:7–10', *Interpretation* 12 (1958), pp. 39–51, p. 48. Omark argues that, if Jesus had avoided death, he would have missed 'the achievement of his mission', and would have forfeited his relationship with God. O'Brien, *Hebrews*, p. 199, notes that *ek thanatou* means that God delivered Jesus 'out of the realm or power of death' through resurrection and exaltation (cf. 13:20).

as portrayed in Isaiah 50:4–9; 53:3–12 (Heb. 7:27; 9:28). Experiences prior to the cross were designed to elicit and test the reality of the obedience that ultimately achieved the will of God for the sanctification and perfection of his people (10:5–14). However, so that he might be a merciful high priest who is able to 'sympathize with our weaknesses' and offer appropriate help to those who are being tested (4:15–16; cf. 2:17–18; 12:1–4), it was necessary for him to experience 'just what obedience to God involved in practice, in the conditions of human life on earth.'[17] Jesus was perfected in the sense of being vocationally qualified, rather than being morally perfected or perfected in his humanity.

Qualified as high priest of a better covenant

The final reference to the perfecting of Jesus (7:28) comes in a context where the focus is on his heavenly exaltation, and only brief mention is made of his sacrifice (7:27) and the personal qualities that make him superior to any earthly mediators (7:26). Nevertheless, these verses reflect what has already been said about the perfecting of Jesus through earthly struggles, death, resurrection and ascension (2:10; 5:7–9).

The statement in 7:28 comes at the end of the writer's extended comparison between the ministry of Levitical priests under the old covenant and the messianic priesthood of Jesus 'after the order of Melchizedek', as promised in Psalm 110:4. Hebrews 8 – 10 goes on to expound the way his ministry inaugurates and fulfils the promises of the new covenant, as set forth in Jeremiah 31:31–34. So the reference to the perfecting of the Son in 7:28 is resumptive, and not the main point of the argument at this stage. Indeed, the writer tells us that the main point is that 'we have such a high priest, one who

---

17. F. F. Bruce, *The Epistle to the Hebrews*, NICNT (Grand Rapids: Eerdmans, 1964), p. 103. Cf. Peterson, *Hebrews and Perfection*, pp. 94–103. The passive use of the verb in 5:9, 7:28 continues the idea from 2:10 that the Son is perfected by the Father in his role as saviour-high priest: the perfecting of Christ involves more than his own self-consecration to the Father's will.

is seated at the right hand of the Majesty in heaven, a minister in the holy places, in the true tent that the Lord set up, not man' (8:1–2). These ideas are developed in the chapters that follow.

In 7:11–19 the claim is made that if perfection had been attainable through the Levitical priesthood and the provisions of the Mosaic law, there would have been no need for God to promise a new priestly order in Psalm 110:4. The perfecting of believers will be discussed below, but first it is necessary to understand how the promise of eternal priesthood is fulfilled. Fundamentally, we are told that Jesus became a priest, 'not on the basis of a legal require-ment concerning bodily descent', as were those who succeeded Aaron, 'but by the power of an indestructible life' (7:16). This last expression refers to his resurrection-ascension, by which he was 'exalted above the heavens' (7:26) and made 'a priest forever, after the order of Melchizedek' (7:17).[18]

The focus in 7:20–28 is on the divine oath in Psalm 110:4 that confirms the eternity of Jesus' priesthood and makes him 'guarantor of a better covenant' (7:22; cf. 8:6; 9:15; 12:24). As distinct from the former priests, who were 'prevented by death from continuing in office', Jesus 'holds his priesthood permanently, because he continues forever' (7:23–24). This is the essential significance of the priesthood 'after the order of Melchizedek'. In practical terms, it means that the exalted Jesus 'is able to save to the uttermost those who draw near to God through him, since *he always lives to make intercession for them*' (7:25).[19]

---

18. The expression cannot refer to the union of the divine and human in the incarnation, since Jesus' earthly life experienced destruction through death. He acquired a new quality of life through heavenly exaltation and in this way 'became' high priest after the order of Melchizedek. Cf. Peterson, *Hebrews and Perfection*, pp. 110–111, 191–195.

19. The expression *sōzein eis to panteles dynatai* could be translated 'able for all time to save' (NRSV), though this is a less natural reading of the Greek syntax than ESV or TNIV ('able to save completely'). The notion of Christ's continuing intercession reflects the perspective of the pivotal exhortations in 4:14–16; 10:19–25. Cf. Peterson, *Hebrews and Perfection*, pp. 114–116.

Three adjectives are used to describe the qualities of Jesus as high priest in 7:26 ('holy, innocent, unstained'), explaining why his sacrifice was so perfect, needing no repetition (7:27; cf. 9:14). The next clause ('separated from sinners') could extend this description, but it is more likely to be linked with what follows ('exalted above the heavens'). Jesus, who remained obedient and faithful to his Father through great testing, is now separated from the realm of sin through resurrection and ascension. The perfection of his sacrifice is associated with the perfection of the victim: he has no need, like the Levitical priests, 'to offer sacrifices daily, first for his own sins and then for those of the people, since he did this once for all when he offered up himself' (7:27).

In 7:28, the law is contrasted with 'the word of the oath, which came later than the law', meaning the sworn promise of God in Psalm 110:4. The point is also made that the law 'appoints men in their weakness as high priests', but the word of the oath 'appoints a Son who has been made perfect for ever'. Many high priests are contrasted with the one enduring high priest of the new covenant (as in 7:23–25) and their human weakness is contrasted with 'a Son who has been made perfect for ever' (as in 7:26–27; cf. 5:2–3). Reference to the perfecting of Jesus as Son recalls 5:8–9 and the preceding argument that the Son enters his inheritance through suffering and heavenly exaltation (1:3–13; 2:5–9). As the incarnate Son, 'he learned obedience through what he suffered', offered himself as the perfect sacrifice for sin, and was raised to sit at God's 'right hand' in fulfilment of Psalm 110:1 (Heb. 1:3–4, 13; 10:12–13; 12:2). As in 5:5–6, his exaltation as Son is associated with his appointment as 'a priest forever, after the order of Melchizedek'.[20]

---

20. Hebrews does not focus on changes involved in the 'being' of Christ through heavenly exaltation but on the consequences of his death, resurrection-ascension and enthronement for his people. The perfecting of Christ is vocationally, rather than metaphysically presented. Cf. Peterson, *Hebrews and Perfection*, pp. 119–125.

The perfecting of believers

The weakness of the law and its priesthood

Perfection in relation to believers is first mentioned in a section beginning with the use of the cognate noun *teleiōsis* (7:11, 'if perfection had been attainable through the Levitical priesthood') and ending with the use of the verb (7:19, 'for the law made nothing perfect'). The fact that Psalm 110 predicted the coming of a messiah-priest 'after the order of Melchizedek' implied a weakness in the existing order. When Jesus appeared 'in the likeness of Melchizedek', 'not on the basis of a legal requirement concerning bodily descent, but by the power of an indestructible life' (7:15–16), it was plain that a better way of relating to God had been provided.

Perfection was neither possible through the Levitical priesthood nor through the whole legal system that was based on that priesthood. The specific commandment that is 'set aside because of its weakness and uselessness' (7:18) is the one requiring a particular 'bodily descent' for ordination to the priesthood (7:16). But the writer extends his negative argument to the law of Moses as a whole ('for the law made nothing perfect'), and introduces the positive note that in the high priestly ministry of Jesus a better hope is introduced, 'through which we draw near to God' (7:19, *di' hēs engizomen tō theō*).[21]

The argument of this verse is developed more fully in chapters 8 – 10, but the simple contrast here gives an important indication of what the writer means by the perfecting of believers. All the institutions of the law, such as priesthood, sacrifice and tabernacle, failed to bring about the access to God and security of fellowship with God that Jesus makes possible under the new covenant. A link between drawing near to God and perfection is also made in 10:1,

---

21. The verb *engizein* is used in the LXX for priestly ministry (e.g. Exod. 19:21–22; Lev. 10:3; 21:21), and more generally for the approach of all God's people to him in prayer or cultic worship (e.g. Gen. 18:23; Eccl. 4:17 [ET 5:1]; Isa. 29:13; 58:2). Cf. Peterson, *Hebrews and Perfection*, p. 246, n. 49.

where it is argued that the law, having only 'a shadow of the good things to come instead of the true form of these realities', can never, by the same sacrifices that are continually offered every year, 'make perfect those who draw near to God' (*tous proserchomenous teleiōsai*). Using parallel terminology, this verse implies that drawing near to God was possible through the provisions of the law, but only in a limited way. Those who would draw near to God can only be perfected in that endeavour through Christ and his saving work (10:14; 12:22–24).[22]

This suggests that the verb *teleioun* is being used consistently throughout Hebrews in a vocational way. Jesus is perfected as saviour and messianic high priest and his people are perfected as those who draw near to God through him. His perfecting makes their perfecting possible.[23] Jesus achieves this by introducing 'a better hope' (7:19), that is based on the 'better covenant' of which he is guarantor (7:22) and mediator (8:6; 12:24). The new covenant is enacted on better promises (8:6) and is eternal in its consequences (13:20). The final goal of the relationship with God that Jesus makes possible is to share his glory (2:10), to enter God's rest (4:11), to see the Lord (12:14), and to inhabit the heavenly city (12:22; 13:14).

Nevertheless, despite the unfulfilled aspect of this relationship, drawing near to God though Jesus is very much a present possibility

22. The verb *proserchesthai* is more commonly used in Hebrews (4:16; 7:25; 10:1, 22; 11:6; 12:18, 22) than *engizein* (7:19). In the LXX, it is used to describe all Israel coming before the Lord in solemn assembly (e.g. Exod. 16:9; 34:32; Num. 10:3–4), and the special role of priests approaching the altar with sacrifices (e.g. Lev. 9:7–8; 22:3). Sirach 1:28, 30; 2:1 expresses the more general sense of relating to God by serving him. In Heb. 11:6, the person who would draw near to God is the one who seeks him by faith. In 7:25, Christ the heavenly high priest is able to save to the uttermost 'those who draw near to God through him'.

23. Scholer, *Proleptic Priests*, p. 199, rightly observes that 'the agent who effects perfection is Jesus, whereas believers realize perfection by "drawing near"'. However, as mentioned in note 12 above, Scholer inadequately equates the perfecting of Jesus with his heavenly exaltation.

(7:19, 25). Christians have already 'drawn near' to God in the New Jerusalem (12:22, *proselēlythate* [perfect tense]). They are members of the heavenly assembly (12:23) because they have come to God through Jesus, 'the mediator of a new covenant' (12:24). At the same time, because of the ongoing struggle with temptation and the need to persevere in faith, hope and love, they are literally urged to 'keep on drawing near to God' (4:16; 10:22, *proserchōmetha* [present tense]) through the high-priestly intercession of Jesus (7:25; 8:1–2). The 'better hope' by which Christians draw near to God is not simply the hope of future resurrection: it is the *present* hope that Jesus gives of approaching God 'with confidence' (4:16, *meta parrēsias*; cf. 10:19), so as to be sustained in that relationship until final glorification. 'The certainty of the actualization of the drawing near is now stronger and surer and more complete than in the OT and later Judaism.'[24]

Cleansed to serve

At the end of a section outlining the weaknesses of the Mosaic covenant and its regulations for worship (9:1–10), Hebrews highlights the inability of material gifts and sacrifices literally 'to perfect the worshipper with respect to conscience' (*kata syneidēsin teleiōsai ton latreuonta*). Such rituals 'deal only with food and drink and various washings, regulations for the body imposed until the time of reformation'.

Although the Greek can be translated to 'perfect the conscience of the worshipper', it is important to understand that the verb *teleiōsai* has 'the worshipper' as its direct object and that *kata syneidēsin* ('with respect to conscience') signifies a particular sphere in which this perfecting must take place. So the writer once more uses the verb in a vocational sense, this time with reference to those who would worship or serve God (*latreuein*, as in 9:14; 10:2; 12:28). An interesting parallel occurs in 10:1–2, where the writer points out that the sacrifices of the old covenant cannot 'make perfect those who draw near' (*tous proserchomenous teleiōsai*), and then observes, 'otherwise, would

---

24. H. Preisker, *TDNT*, vol. 2, p. 331.

they not have ceased to be offered, since the worshippers [*tous latreuontas*] having once been cleansed, would no longer have any consciousness of sin [*syneidēsin hamartiōn*]'.[25] It is the cleansing of the conscience that makes possible the perfecting of the worshipper, according to the next section of the argument (9:11–14).

With the appearance of Christ as 'a high priest of the good things that have come', what was foreshadowed in the Old Testament has become a reality. Jesus has definitively fulfilled the role of the high priest on the annual Day of Atonement (9:7, 11–12; Lev 16:1–19). When he ascended 'through the heavens' (4:14), he passed through 'the greater and more perfect tent (not made with hands, that is, not of this creation)', opening the way into the heavenly sanctuary or 'heaven itself' (9:11, 24; cf. 8:1–2). Jesus did not enter the heavenly presence of God 'by means of the blood of goats and calves but by means of his own blood' (9:12). Since his sacrifice was so perfect he entered the Most Holy Place 'once for all', thus securing 'an eternal redemption'. A similar expression in 9:15 indicates freedom from the judgment and guilt produced by sin, so 'eternal redemption' is another way of speaking about the once-for-all and standing offer of forgiveness promised in Jeremiah 31:34 (Heb. 8:12; 10:17–18).

Outlining the practical consequences of Christ's death, 9:13–14 asserts that ritual cleansing under the old covenant was for the benefit of those who were ceremonially unclean, to sanctify them by making them outwardly clean (*pros tēn tēs sarkos katharotēta*, 'for the purification of the flesh'). Those who were defiled could only be restored to fellowship with God in the sense that they were able to participate again in the worship of the Israelite community. The fundamental truth that blood 'purifies' and 'sanctifies', even if only at an external level, provides the basis for the 'how much more'

25. Although Hebrews is more sparing in its use of *syneidēsis* (9:9, 14; 10:2, 22; 13:18) than Paul, these references show how central the concept is to the writer's thinking. C. Maurer, *TDNT*, vol. 7, pp. 898–919, rightly argues that OT teaching about the heart must be taken into account when evaluating what the NT means by conscience. Cf. Peterson, *Hebrews and Perfection*, pp. 134–136.

argument that follows. 'The blood of Christ' is uniquely effective because he 'offered himself without blemish to God', alluding once more to Jesus' life of perfect obedience to the Father, culminating in the cross (cf. 5:7–9; 7:26–27; 10:10).[26] His sacrifice is able to 'purify our conscience from dead works', meaning sins that defile the conscience and bring judgment, so that we might 'serve the living God'. A true and lasting consecration to God and his service is thus implied.

The new covenant promise of a renewed 'heart', based on a decisive forgiveness of sins (Jer. 31:33–34), is echoed here. Only the cleansing provided by Jesus Christ can set believers free to serve the living God in the way that Jeremiah predicted. A later challenge to 'offer to God acceptable worship' (12:28–29), followed by a sequence of exhortations to live holy, loving and obedient lives (13:1–16), shows how the worship of the new covenant is meant to be expressed in every sphere of life.[27]

Perfection and sanctification

Hebrews further outlines the limitations of the law and its provisions for approaching God in 10:1–4, characterizing these as 'a shadow of the good things to come instead of the true form of these realities' (10:1; cf. 8:5). Psalm 40:6–8 is then used to establish that the whole sacrificial system is replaced by the perfectly obedient self-offering of Christ (10:5–10). The result is that, by God's will, 'we have been sanctified through the offering of the body of Jesus Christ once for all' (10:10). His once-for-all sacrifice (*ephapax*) brings the once-for-all cleansing from sin that the law could not provide (10:2, *hapax*). Such cleansing makes possible a decisive consecration or positional sanctification of believers to God (*hēgiasmenoi esmen*; cf. 10:29; 13:12,

---

26. 'Through the eternal Spirit' most likely refers to the power of the Holy Spirit upholding and maintaining him (cf. Isa. 42:1), though some would take it to mean his own spirit, highlighting the interior or spiritual quality of his sacrifice.

27. Cf. D. G. Peterson, *Engaging with God: A Biblical Theology of Worship* (Leicester: Apollos, 1992), pp. 241–246.

'through his own blood').[28] In this way, the writer suggests the fulfilment of the promise that God would put his laws 'on their hearts'
and write them 'on their minds', because he would 'remember their
sins and their lawless deeds no more' (Jer. 31:33–4; Heb. 10:16–17).
Such dedication to God and his service is achieved for us by Jesus
Christ, in whom heart-obedience was perfectly expressed.

In contrast with the priests of the old covenant, who stand daily
at the altar to offer 'repeatedly the same sacrifices, which can never
take away sins', Jesus sits at God's right hand, his sacrificial work
completed (10:11–14). The result is that by a single offering 'he has
perfected for all time those who are being sanctified (*teteleiōken eis to
diēnekes tous hagiazomenous*)'. The Greek grammar stresses that perfection is accomplished by Christ's sacrifice in the past, and that the
benefits are permanently enjoyed by those who are perfected as
'the sanctified'.[29]

Perfection and glorification

Although Hebrews 11 mentions many who are commended in
Scripture for their faith, the writer nevertheless concludes that they
'did not receive what was promised' (11:39). God's people under the
old covenant saw the fulfilment of specific promises in this life (e.g.,
6:15; 11:11, 33), but none of them experienced the blessings of the
messianic era and of the new covenant. The writer explains this in
terms of God's gracious provision for his readers: 'since God had
planned something better for us, that apart from us they should
not be made perfect' (11:40). Put another way, God reserved the
messianic perfection until we could share in it!

---

28. Cf. D. G. Peterson, *Possessed by God: A New Testament Theology of
Sanctification and Holiness*, NSBT 1 (Leicester: Apollos, 1995), pp. 33–40.

29. As in 2:11, the present tense of the substantive participle (*tous
hagiazomenous*) is best read as a timeless designation of those who
benefit from the saving death of Jesus. Sanctification, which is
definitively effected by his blood (10:10, 29: 13:12), makes it possible
to draw near to God with confidence and worship God acceptably.
Cf. Peterson, *Hebrews and Perfection*, pp. 150–153.

It is not necessary to give the verb *teleioun* a different sense here, relating it only to glorification. Hebrews attributes the totality of the messianic salvation to the high-priestly work of Jesus in his death and heavenly exaltation. Expressed in terms of the Christian's access to the heavenly sanctuary, our present experience of drawing near with confidence is the assurance of ultimate transfer to the presence of God in the heavenly city (6:19–20; 9:15; 12:22–24).[30] According to 10:14, the sanctified are perfected 'for all time'. In his own perfecting, Jesus has done what is necessary to bring believers to glory (cf. Rom. 8:30).

Men and women of faith under the old covenant looked forward to life in the heavenly city (11:10, 13–16), but those who come to God through the mediation of Jesus Christ (12:22, *proselēlythate*) are now part of that joyful assembly. In the heavenly Jerusalem, the ultimate company of the people of God is identified as 'the assembly of the firstborn who are enrolled in heaven'. They are also described as 'the spirits of the righteous made perfect' (12:23, *pneumasi dikaiōn teteleiōmenōn*).[31] The terminology of perfection here recalls the promise of 10:14. Other facets of the preceding argument are recalled when the writer describes Jesus as 'the mediator of a new covenant' and his 'sprinkled blood' as speaking 'a better word than the blood of Abel'. The blood of Jesus offers the possibility of complete cleansing from the defilement of sin (9:13–15; 10:22), giving open access to 'God the judge of all' (12:23) and life for ever in his presence.

---

30. In 9:15 it is clear that the death of Jesus has a retrospective effect for believers 'under the first covenant', but 11:39–40 indicates that they did not experience the benefits of this in their lifetime. See also note 29.

31. Both expressions should be understood in a comprehensive way to describe believers under both old and new covenants, who finally enjoy the inheritance promised to God's children, now secured for them by Jesus as the Son and messianic high priest. So 12:23 speaks of the fulfilment of 11:40. Cf. Peterson, *Hebrews and Perfection*, pp. 162–166.

Perfection and maturity

In an exhortation preceding the central doctrinal section of Hebrews, the writer expresses his concern that the readers have become 'dull of hearing' and are unprepared to receive the teaching he is about to impart (5:11–12). They are immature, desiring only 'milk', whereas 'the mature' thrive on 'solid food', having their powers of discernment 'trained by constant practice to distinguish good from evil' (5:13–14). Although the adjective *teleios* ('mature') is clearly a cognate of the verb *teleioun*, it is not used here as part of the writer's argument about the perfecting of believers. Maturity and perfection are two different, but related strands of thought in Hebrews.

As we have seen, perfection is achieved for us by the perfecting of Christ. Perfection is the gift of God to those who draw near to him through Jesus, on the basis of his once-for-all sacrifice and heavenly exaltation. In contrast with *nēpios* ('child'), *teleios* describes a person who has grown spiritually and morally through careful attention to Christian teaching, applying what is learnt in everyday life and relationships.[32] The related noun is used in 6:1, in the writer's warning to 'leave the elementary doctrine of Christ and go on to maturity' (*tēn teleiotēta*).

Nevertheless, teaching about perfection is central to the solid food that the writer seeks to impart. Properly understood, it provides the greatest encouragement to faith and zeal. Such teaching is not only appropriate for the mature, but is used by the writer to draw the immature along the pathway to maturity. Just as children are encouraged to grow physically by feeding them more and more solid food, so the writer intends to mature his readers by his profound teaching. What he says about perfection should encourage them to be confident about their relationship with God and to persevere in that confidence, even in the face of hostility and suffering.

Such is the emphasis in the final passage where this terminology is found. Challenging them to follow the example of the great 'cloud

---

32. Cf. Peterson, *Hebrews and Perfection*, pp. 176–187.

of witnesses' in chapter 11 and 'lay aside every weight, and sin which clings so closely', the writer exhorts them to 'run with endurance the race that is set before us' (12:1). However, the Christian has the added advantage of being able to look to Jesus, who is literally 'the pioneer and perfecter of faith' (12:2, *ton tēs pisteōs archēgon kai teleiōtēn*). As in 2:10, the noun *archēgos* appears to be used with a double meaning: Jesus is both the *source* of persevering faith in his saving work and the *pioneer*, who blazes the trail for us to follow on our journey to the heavenly city ('who for the joy that was set before him endured the cross, despising the shame, and is seated at the right hand of God').

When Jesus is described as the 'perfecter of faith', a rare noun is used in Greek (*teleiōtēn*), probably formed from the verb. Formally, the expression means that Jesus makes possible a true realization of faith in God. His own faith was qualitatively, and not just quantitatively greater than the faith of Old Testament saints. By the exercise of his own faith, he has given our faith a perfect basis in his high priestly work, achieving our salvation by his obedience. At the same time, he has opened the way for his people to follow him through suffering and shame to the Father's presence. The grace of God in the work of Christ is the basis for a true confidence in God and his promises, encouraging believers to persevere in faith, hope and love, until they experience the fullness of everything that Jesus has already accomplished for them.

8. SUFFERING WITH THE SAVIOUR

THE REALITY, THE REASONS AND THE REWARD

Bruce W. Winter

The recipients of the epistle to the Hebrews had initially suffered severely for their new-found faith and at the time of the writing there had arisen the threat of further suffering. The description of it succinctly recorded in 10:32–34 shows how intense it was and the extremely high cost incurred for confessing the perpetual divinity of Jesus as the Son of God and his central role as the great high priest.

The temptation to avoid ongoing suffering by compromising their beliefs and possibly sheltering under the umbrella of Judaism may have seemed the way to evade. The writer of this letter feared that this would end in apostasy. His deep concern shapes important themes of this remarkable letter, not least the theme of suffering.

This chapter will first trace the details of the suffering the recipients of the letter had endured and one they were about to face, and then the reasons for this (both from Roman law and the expected expressions of Roman loyalty), and finally the arguments mounted by the writer in favour of not shrinking back from suffering, but enduring further adversity because of the ultimate reward.

The reality of suffering

The writer does not underplay past suffering. He records that they 'had endured much conflict of sufferings' (*pollēn athlēsin hypemeinate pathēmatōn*) 10:32.[1] The term 'conflict' evokes a combative image and was appropriately borrowed from ancient sporting contests that were sometimes linked to war in Greek thinking.[2] Hebrews 10:32–34 catalogues what this involved for these Christians when they were first 'enlightened' by the gospel. The word 'sufferings' is in the plural and the writer gives four helpful indicators of what they were.

Verbal abuse in the theatre

He records that this was not a private experience but was a 'public exposure' in the one place where this happened in the ancient world – the theatre. The term *theatrizō* used here means 'to put on stage', i.e., 'public display' (10:33).[3] The verb is in the passive in order to indicate that what happened was not of their volition but was forced on them. A hostile audience assembled in the theatre hurled 'insulting abuses' at the Christians.

A similar event is recorded in Acts 19:21–41 where first-century Christians and Paul's fellow workers, Gaius and Aristarchus, were

---

1. Unless noted otherwise, translations of the New Testament and other ancient literature are my own.
2. Z. Newby, *Athletics in the Ancient World* (London: Bristol Classical Press, 2006), pp. 71–72, 93. Their trainers sometimes beat them with whips, see the vase painting in Newby, *Athletics*, p. 72, plate 14. *LS* records the term means 'contest', 'combat', especially of athletes 'in the athletic competitions' (see *LS* for sources). They also cite use of this word in Heb. 10:32 to refer generally to a 'struggle', 'trial'.
3. For the use of this term 'expose to public shame' see Polybius, *Histories*, 11.8.7. For a cognate *ektheatrizō* 'make a public show of', Polybius, ibid. 3.91.10. Paul also used the cognate *theatron* metaphorically where traditionally criminals were sentenced to death by public execution as entertainment of the citizens in the theatre. See V. H. Nguyen, 'The Identification of Paul's Spectacle of Death Metaphor in 1 Corinthians 4:9', *NTS* 53 (2007), pp. 489–501.

dragged into the theatre in Ephesus (which seated over 20,000 people). The purpose was to humiliate them in such a way that it would discredit their faith before a vast number of Ephesian citizens. This was instigated by Demetrius the silversmith, who had incited his fellow tradesmen to stir up the city against the Christians with the affirmation 'Great is Artemis of the Ephesians' (Acts 19:23–28). When Alexander, who was 'Jewish', 'motioned with his hand, wishing to make a defence to the people', the crowd was further incited and shouted for about two hours 'Great is Artemis of the Ephesians'. Some Christians, along with the Asiarchs, leading authorities and friends of Paul, convinced him not to venture into the theatre as it was so dangerous (Acts 19:30–31). The intention of this public spectacle was to subject Gaius and Aristarchus to public shame and physical harm, thereby denigrating the Christian message.

Public scourging

Unlike Paul's two fellow workers in Ephesus who escaped suffering through the intervention of the civic official, young Hebrew converts actually experienced publicly 'verbal abuses (*oneidismois*) and also (*te kai*) physical punishments (*thlipsesis*)', i.e., floggings (10:33).

In an illuminating parallel, Philo of Alexandria related how Aulus Avilius Flaccus, Prefect of Egypt AD 32–38, humiliated Alexandrian Jews by having them stripped naked and scourged in a public 'spectacle' in the theatre.

> '[He] arranged a splendid procession to send through the middle of the market-place a body of old men prisoners, with their hands bound, some with thongs and others with iron chains, whom he led in this plight into the theatre, a most miserable spectacle, and incongruous with the occasion. And then he commanded them all to stand in front of their enemies, who were sitting down, to make their disgrace the more conspicuous, and ordered them all to be stripped of their clothes and scourged with stripes, in a way that only the most wicked of criminals are usually treated, and they were flogged with such severity that some of

them the moment they were carried out died of their wounds, while others were rendered so ill for a long time that their recovery was despaired of.[4]

Philo goes on to record how this 'show' (*thea*) had been carefully staged. '[T]he first of the public spectacles [*theamatōn*]' were physical punishments of naked Jews in 'the middle of the orchestra [pit] [*orchēstras*]' that would last 'from the morning to the third or fourth hour' and then they would be dragged off to their execution through the theatre. He then recounts derisively 'and after this beautiful exhibition came the dancers, and the buffoons, and the flute-players, and all the other diversions of the theatrical contests'.[5] Josephus also succinctly records how Jews were physically punished in the theatre and then put to death.[6] The experience of both public abuse and physical beatings meted out to the early Christian converts had been severe.

Imprisonment

Their sufferings were not short-lived, for they had also been incarcerated. The text indicates Christians 'became partners with those treated thus' (*koinōnoi tōn houtōs anastrephomemōn genēthentes*, 10:33b). This is further explained, 'For you also had compassion on the prisoners' (10:34a). Later they are required to remember those in prison who are described as 'fellow prisoners' (*syndedemenoi*) and those who are ill-treated (*tōn kakouchoumenōn*, 13:3), i.e., who suffered 'abuse and afflictions' (10:33). Life in prison in the first century did not simply involve loss of freedom. Conditions were generally harsh and especially so when the prisoner had no sustenance from those outside.[7]

---

4. Philo, *Flaccus* 74–75.

5. Ibid., 84–85.

6. Josephus, *Against Apion*, 1.43.

7. B. Rapske, *Paul in Roman Custody, The Book of Acts in its First Century Setting*, 3 vols. (Grand Rapids: Eerdmans, 1994), vol. 3, pp. 14–15.

Confiscation of property

There was yet another blow. There were substantial personal losses with 'the seizure of your properties' (*harpagē tōn hypagrchontōn hymōn*, 10:34b). It is suggested that the property of the Christians to whom he is writing was not plundered by any mob, but was acquired legally as a further substantial penalty. Saller has argued that the house in many ways defined the family.[8] When faced with a potential loss of his property through legal processes Cicero asked, 'What is more sacred, what is more protected by all religion than the house of each and every citizen?'[9] Therefore this punishment was intended to be a bitter blow to these Christians.

Impending exile

Exile with Christ 'outside the camp' is the immediate threat hanging over their heads (13:11–14). Just as under the Jewish law 'the sacrifice for sins are burnt outside the camp, so also Jesus suffered outside the gate [of the city]'. On this basis, 'So then [*toinun*] we must go forth to him outside the camp and bear the abuse he endured ['abuse' is the same word used for what the Christians had originally endured in 10:33]. For we have no lasting city, but we seek the city that is to come' (13:13–14). The inferential particle followed by the hortatory subjunctive in 13:14 suggests that exile was pending and, while this was a terrible disgrace in the first century, it would be acceptable for Christians, given their eternal dwelling (see 13:14).

It seems that the Roman sword was still hanging over their heads with the threat of exile to a distant place, an island, or 'to the most desert part' of their province, to cite the Roman legal code, *The Digest* (see below). It was bad enough to have to have been humiliated, whipped, deprived of property and to become ex-prisoners, but the insecurity and the consequences of exile with all its unknowns must have seemed the final straw, perhaps even a

---

8. R. P. Saller, *Patriarch, Property and Death in the Roman Family* (Cambridge, Cambridge University Press, 1994), ch. 4.
9. Cicero, *De domo suo*, 108.

price too high to pay. In that light, the search for a way out is explicable.

This catalogue of punishments reflects a development in the way punishments prescribed in Roman law were administered at that time. Aubert has drawn attention to a development in Roman criminal law in the time of Nero when 'legislators devised new and harsher penalties, such as hard labour, mandatory exile and deportation to an island'. He also notes, 'Roman magistrates had acquired some leeway in the interpretation of the law' and they also blurred the punishments of different penalties for different social classes. He calls this trend the 'discrepancy or congruence, between theory and practice in Roman criminal law and practice'.[10] This explains the multiple punishments these Christians had experienced and what was pending.

The reasons for sufferings

This section seeks to unlock the reasons for extreme, multiple punishments of Christians and the pressure they were feeling at the time of the writing of this letter. The first relates to Roman law, the other to the conflict between loyalty to Christ and the cultic expressions of loyalty to Rome.

Roman law

In the case of an indictable offence, Roman law prescribed that 'the property of those who ought to be accused, or have been caught committing a crime, or who have killed themselves should be confiscated [by the Treasury]'. It goes to declare that 'the property

---

10. J.-J. Aubert, 'A Double Standard in Roman Criminal Law? The Death Penalty and Social Structure in Late Republic and Early Roman Empire', in J.-J. Aubert and B. Sirks (eds.), *Specvlum Ivris: Roman Law as a Reflection of Social and Economic Life in Antiquity* (Ann Arbor: University of Michigan Press, 2002), pp. 94–133, pp. 103, 105.

of anyone who kills himself after he has been accused should be confiscated by the Treasury only where he was accused of a crime for which, if he were convicted, he should be punished with death or deportation'.[11]

Had the Christians committed a criminal offence? Rapkse in his discussion of 'prison and coercion' notes that 'since legal provisions kept magistrates from using the most severe forms of *coercitio* upon citizens, imprisonment was used instead'. This applied not only to the earlier Roman Republic but also to the empire as well. He records, 'It [imprisonment] was also a recourse of magistrates to compel the obedience of individuals of lesser stature in Roman eyes – namely, foreigners, slaves and women'.[12] Was their imprisonment 'to compel their obedience' and the sequestration of their property something undertaken within the provision 'ought to be punished'?

Were there legal charges upon which Christians could be indicted? That early Christians should face situations of conflict with the ruling authorities does not surprise ancient historians. O. F. Robinson, Reader in Law, University of Glasgow, in her book *The Criminal Law of Ancient Rome* devotes chapter 6 to 'Offenses against the State' with a discussion of 'treason' and 'sedition', and to the official repression of '*collegia*', i.e., 'associations'. Under the legislation enacted by Augustus, Christians could not legally meet weekly, even though Jews were permitted to do so. The rule for all other groups, including '*collegia*' (associations), was that 'regular meetings were to be no more than monthly'; '[T]his is one reason why Christians could hardly have formed legal *collegia*, since they need to meet weekly for worship.'[13]

In the eyes of first-century emperors, governors and ruling authorities in cities of the empire, *collegia* 'represented a threat to

11. *The Digest*, ed. Scott, XLVIII, 21.3.1.
12. Rapske, *Paul in Roman Custody*, pp. 14–16.
13. O. F. Robinson, *The Criminal Law of Ancient Rome* (London: Duckworth, 1995), p. 80.

Roman order rather than a standing offence, but they could be repressed severely; accusations were made before the Prefect of the City'.[14] In *Lex Irnitus*, a city constitution uncovered recently, there is the following law described as 'Concerning illegal gatherings, societies and colleges (*collegia*)'.

> No one is to take part in an illegal gathering [*coetum facito*] in that *municipium* [self-governing town] or to hold a meeting of a society or college for that purpose or to conspire that it be held or to act in such a way that any of these things occur. Anyone who acts contrary to these rules is to be condemned to pay 10,000 *secterces* to the *municipes* of the *Municipium Flavium Irnitanum* and the right of action, suit and claim of that money and concerning that money is to belong to any *municipes* of that *Municipium*.[15]

J. Gonzalez, the editor of this bronze inscription, makes this significant comment on this constitution: 'It is important to observe that the only thing actually banned is a *coetus*', i.e., 'assembly'.[16]

In a much earlier constitution, *Lex coloniae Genetiae Juliae* (45 BC) the incomplete section CVI records, 'No colonist of the colony [Roman] Genetiva, established by order of G. Caesar the dictator, shall (get together) any assemblage or meeting or conspiracy'. According to Hardy who was its editor, 'These would come under the category of *majestas*', i.e., 'treason'.[17]

It is significant that all the Julio-Claudian emperors saw some associations as hotbeds for fermenting political dissents and therefore a thorn in their side. But at a provincial and civic level

---

14. Ibid.

15. The *Lex Irnitus*, ch. 74. For the text see J. Gonzalez, 'The *Lex Irnitus*: A New Flavian Municipal Law', *JRS* LXXVI (1986), pp. 147–243, p. 193.

16. Ibid., p. 223.

17. E. G. Hardy, *Three Spanish Charters and Other Documents* (Oxford: Clarendon Press, 1912), p. 50, n. 121, citing *The Digest* XLVIII, 4.1.2.

some did function beneficially provided they operated within the parameters set by Roman law.[18]

The synagogue was the exception provided for under the Augustan legislation for controlling associations. The Jews as an ethnic group could legally assemble there once a week. Others could legally meet only once a month. Did the Christian movement qualify? In the province of Achaea one of the implications of the legal ruling of the noted jurist, Gallio,[19] would have allowed for this; he emphatically declared that the issues brought before him were a matter of 'the law, your law' (Acts 18:12–17).[20] His *imperium* did not go beyond his province and therefore could not legalize weekly gatherings of Christians everywhere in the empire.

The prohibition about meetings may throw light on the exhortation in 10:25 'not to neglect the meeting together [*episynagōgē*] as is the habit of some'. The reason for absence is not given but it could have been that some Christians realized that attendance on a weekly basis was contrary to the law.

One of the legal duties of the proconsul of a province relating to 'relegation [*relagatio*] and property of offenders' was to exile certain offenders. It legislated that 'exile is of a threefold nature; interdiction

---

18. For evidence of this with Augustus, Tiberius, Claudius and Nero see B. W. Winter, 'The Imperial Cult and the Early Christians in Pisidian Antioch (Acts 13 and Galatians 6)', in T. Drew-Bear, M. Tashalan and C. M. Thomas (eds.), *Acts du 1ᵉʳ Congres International sur Antioche de Pisidie* (Lyon: Université Lumière-Lion, 2002), pp. 67–75, pp. 72–74. For primary sources where some associations connect with civic good will and imperial powers, see also P. A. Harland, 'Honouring the Emperor or Assailing of the Beast: Participation in Civic Life Among Associations (Jewish, Christian and Other) in Asia Minor and the Apocalypse of John', *JSNT* 22.77 (2000), pp. 99–121, pp. 110–113.

19. For a discussion of the judicial competence of Gallio see B. W. Winter, 'Rehabilitating Gallio and his Judgement in Acts 18:14–15', *TynB*, 57.2 (2006), pp. 291–308.

20. For a discussion of the importance of his decision for Achaean Christians see B. W. Winter, 'Gallio's ruling on the legal status of early Christianity (Acts 18:14–15)', *TynB* 50.2 (1999), pp. 213–224.

of certain places, or of secret flight; or all places are forbidden, except one which is designated; or confinement to one island is prescribed, that is to say, relegation to a single island' or 'to the most desert parts of their provinces'.[21]

Roman loyalty

First-century readers would have been astonished by the opening of the letter to the Hebrews. They would have seen readily that there was an enormous conflict for Christians, faced with Hebrews' divine claims about Jesus and the pressure to show loyalty to the emperor by cultic veneration throughout the year.

This conflict has been commented on by leading ancient historians. In 1972, Fergus Millar, the Emeritus Camden Professor of Ancient History, Oxford University, posed an important question with its inescapable implication: 'But when gentiles began to convert to Christianity, might we not expect that the pagan communities in which they lived would begin to use against them the accusation of not observing the Imperial cult?'[22]

A decade later in a landmark monograph for ancient historians on the imperial cult in the East, Simon Price noted that in a later era 'non-participation by Christians, whose communities were already very widespread in Asia Minor before Constantine, was deeply worrying to the rest of the population. Indeed the problem was already pressing to the assembly of the province of Asia under Hadrian [A.D. 117–138].'[23] Would not this also have been the case for the citizens of the city where these first Christians resided?

---

21. *The Digest* XLVIII, 21.5, 21.7.9.

22. F. Millar, 'The Imperial Cult and the Persecutions', in W. den Boer (ed.), *Le Culte des Souverains dans l'Empire Romain* (Geneva: Vandoeuvres, 1972), pp. 145–165, p. 163.

23. S. R. F. Price, *Rituals and Power: The Imperial Cult and Asia Minor* (Cambridge: Cambridge University Press, 1984), pp. 123–124, citing Eusebius, *Ecclesiastical History*, iv:8–9. See R. A. Horsley, *Paul and Empire: Religion and Power in Roman Imperial Society* (Harrisburg: Trinity Press International, 1997), ch. 3, where its nexus to the first generation of Christians is not explored.

A further decade on, Stephen Mitchell, Professor of Ancient History, University of Exeter, in his extensive work on Anatolia that included the province of Galatia whose capital was Pisidian Antioch, wrote perceptively about the enormous societal pressure that must have existed for early Christian converts to apostatize because of the imperial cult.

> One cannot avoid the impression that the obstacle which stood in the way of the progress of Christianity, and the force which would have drawn new adherents back to conformity with the prevailing paganism, was the public worship of the emperors. The packed calendar of the ruler cult dragooned the citizens of [Pisidian] Antioch into observing the days, months, seasons and years which it laid down for special recognition and celebration . . . it was not a change of heart that might win a Christian convert back to paganism, but the overwhelming pressure to conform imposed by the institutions of his city and the activities of his neighbours.[24]

How did the Christians who are addressed in this letter cope with 'the overwhelming pressure to conform'? All citizens were required to express loyalty to emperors as perpetual divinities, who in the first century were addressed with same titles the Christians used of Jesus.[25] Does this help explain something of the depth of concern in the letter about enormous pressure to commit apostasy that was the inevitable outcome unless Christians were prepared to undergo exile? The very opening of the letter unfolds the unique identity and role of the Son of God, as the heir, the creator, the one who sustains

---

24. S. Mitchell, *Anatolia: Land, Men, and Gods in Asia Minor*, 2 vols. (Oxford: Clarendon Press, 1993), vol. 2, p. 10, *pace* C. Miller, 'The Imperial Cult in the Pauline Cities of Asia Minor and Greece', *CBQ* 72 (2010), pp. 314–332.
25. For primary official sources documenting this see 'Sharing divine titles while "declining" new temples' in my forthcoming monograph, B. W. Winter, *Divine Honours for the Caesars: The First Christians' Responses*, ch. 2.

all things by the word of his power and who, after his apotheosis (i.e. ascension) into heaven, is now seated at the right hand of God (1:2–4). It is significant that this affirmation of perpetual divinity was a claim also made of the emperors in official inscriptions or imperial decrees. Rather than *deus*, a 'deified human being', the term *divis*, 'perpetual divinity', was attributed to Julius Caesar. As Wardle notes, 'The chosen form *Divus Iulius* required relegating his *cognomen* in favour of a *nomen* and juxtaposing a term specifying "god": *C. Iulius Caesares* become *divus Iulius*.'[26]

This indicates a new day for Rome, with the perpetual divinity officially being attributed to Julius Caesar in 41 BC and to living emperors thereafter. In Cyprus a Greek inscription that was dedicated between 9 BC and AD 2 aptly testifies to the succession of imperial divinity, 'To Imperator Caesar Augustus, god, son of god . . . and his two sons, Gaius and Lucius Caesar'. After the death of Augustus and his sons who were his named successors but both of whom died before him, there was later added to the same inscription his actual successor, 'To Tiberius Caesar Augustus, god, son of a god'.[27]

A Latin inscription in the time of Nero sees him as 'Nero Claudius Caesar Augustus Germanicus, son of the divine Claudius (*divi Claudi f.*), grandson of Germanicus Caesar, great-grandson of Tiberius Caesar Augustus, great-great-grandson of the divine Augustus,

---

26. For this important discussion see D. Wardle, '*Deus* or *Divus*: The Genesis of Roman Terminology for Deified Emperors and a Philosopher's Contribution', in G. Clark and T. Rajak (eds.), *Philosophy and Power in the Graeco-Roman World: Essays in Honour of Miriam Griffin* (Oxford: Oxford University Press, 2002), pp. 181–191, p. 191.

27. V. Ehrenberg and A. H. M. Jones, *Documents Illustrating the Reigns of Augustus and Tiberius* (Oxford: Clarendon Press, 1949), no. 115 a and b; see P. Steward, *Statues in Roman Society, Representation and Response* (Oxford: Oxford University Press, 2003), p. 167 for the influence of Latin on the Greek with the different cases supported by bilingual imperial inscriptions.

pontifex maximus . . . ', indicating the perpetual divinity of the step-son of Claudius.[28]

In 63 BC Julius Caesar secured the permanent role of *pontifex maximus* in his lifetime. It meant literally the 'greatest bridge builder', thereby 'making himself the mediator between his fellow-citizens and the state-gods'; 'the office conferred great prestige and paved the way for divine honours'.[29] Augustus assumed the title in 12 BC, as did Tiberius for all his principate and subsequent emperors.[30] For the first-century non-Christian reader of Hebrews, the great high priesthood of Jesus with its beneficial ministry to all Christians discussed in the epistle would be seen as an identical role to that of the reigning emperor – *pontifex maximus* of the entire empire.

The conflict of roles would immediately spring to the mind of any non-Christian reader of Hebrews. Christ's eternal priesthood based on the paradigm of Melchizedek certainly exalted him above any emperor, as did the superiority of his high priestly covenantal role. Similarly, his eternal sanctuary was set over against the many imperial cult temples in the Roman Empire, including Rome.

One response to imperial cultic activities may well be reflected in the letter to the Galatians where in Pisidian Antioch, as in other cities in the province, Jewish Christians themselves were seeking to avoid any persecution for the cross of Christ (Gal. 6:12–14).[31] Paul's response throws light on why the Judaizers placed such enormous pressure (using highly persuasive theological arguments) on Gentile Christians to be circumcised. The reasons had to be persuasive because the foreskin of the male member was regarded as a sign of men's beauty in the first century, and the Romans thought the Jewish

---

28. *Supplementum epigraphicum graecum*, ix, p. 352.
29. D. Fishwick, *The Imperial Cult in the Latin West: Studies in the Ruler Cult of the Western Provinces of the Roman Empire*, 4 vols. (Leiden: E. J. Brill, 1987–2005), vol. 1, p. 56.
30. Ibid., vol. 1, pp. 99, 161.
31. See Winter, 'Imperial Cult', pp. 62–75 and J. K. Hardin, *Galatians and the Imperial Cult: A Critical Analysis of the First-Century Social Context of Paul's Letter*, WUNT II.237 (Tübingen: Mohr Siebeck, 2008), p. 237.

practise 'detestable'.[32] This helps us understand why surgical procedures for restoration for any damage (including the reversal of circumcision, called *epispasm*) were laid down in the medical textbooks.[33] Roman law regarded compelling another man to be circumcised the equivalent to castration, which was a capital offence.[34]

In the earlier chapters of Galatians a great deal of Paul's response is taken up with demolishing the arguments of the 'circumcision' party. There are references to imperial high and holy days and anniversaries around which imperial cultic activities were observed (Gal. 4:10). Paul also records the pressure put on Gentile Christians to become fully Jewish by holding them at arms length unless they agreed to their terms (4:17).[35] Gentile Christians could only come in under their protective Jewish ethnic umbrella if they underwent circumcision and followed Jewish ritual conventions, otherwise they would be excluded and lose the security afforded the Jewish race (4:17).

Claudius had decreed that throughout the empire the Jewish ancient customs and traditions were to be respected and could legally be observed, but they were not to denigrate other religions.[36] Jews had

---

32. First-century Jewish authors record this, e.g., Philo, *Special Laws* 1.2 and Josephus, *Against Apion* 2.13; J. P. V. D. Balsdon, *Romans and Aliens* (London: Duckworth, 1979), p. 216.

33. On the removal with the surgery called *epispasm* see the medical text book of Celsus, *De Medicina* 7:25. This operation is referred to in 1 Cor. 7:18a; see B. W. Winter, *Seek the Welfare of the City: Early Christians as Benefactors and Citizens* (Grand Rapids: Eerdmans, 1994), pp. 147–149.

34. 'Jews are permitted to circumcise only their own children, and anyone who performs this operation upon persons of a different religion [non-Jewish] will incur the penalty of castration.' Modestinus, *Rules*, Book VI.

35. Hardin, *Galatians*, ch. 5.

36. See Josephus, *Jewish Antiquities* 19.5. For a summary from official inscriptions reproduced in *Antiquities* on the Jewish rights allowing them to observe Jewish laws, perform the Jewish cult, and legally assemble, see M. Pucci Ben Zeev, *Jewish Rights in the Roman World: The Greek and Roman Documents Quoted by Flavius Josephus*, Tente und Studien zum Atiken Judentum 74 (Tübingen: Mohr Siebeck, 1995), pp. 375–376.

been offering up a daily sacrifice for the emperor in the temple in Jerusalem. Rajak notes that the Jews were exempt from 'overt participation in emperor worship' and observes at the same time that, unlike the Jews who had special status, 'the early Christians were to lack [this] ... the cities managed to impel the Roman authorities (whose deeper instincts were by no means wholly tolerant when it came to strange oriental cults) to take action against distasteful trouble makers'.[37]

Pressure to conform

Given the hostility of the citizens and the extreme sufferings that the Christians addressed in Hebrews had already undergone, and given the pressures imposed by the veneration of the perpetual divinity of the emperor and his intercessory role as *pontifex maximus* with the gods for the empire, one can appreciate the temptation to shelter under the protective custody of Judaism rather than face exile. As well as the arguments mounted in the letter for the superiority of Jesus, his salvation, ongoing ministry and the superiority of the new covenant over the Jewish one with its cultic practices, the warnings of the enormous and immediate danger of apostasy can be readily understood.

Roman law, as well as Roman loyalty, with its obligatory demands for the performance of cultic honours to the emperor by all the subjects of its vast empire except the Jews, created a problem for these first Christians. It was not dissimilar to the problem faced by a subsequent generation of Christians before the governor Pliny the Younger. He had banned all associations in Pontus because of their suspected anti-Roman stance: 'When people gather together for a common purpose, whatever name we may give them and whatever function we may assign them, they soon become political'.[38] He reported to the emperor, Trajan, his success interrogating some Christians who apostatized.

---

37. T. Rajak, *The Jewish Dialogue with Greece and Rome: Studies in Cultural and Social Interaction* (Leiden: E. J. Brill, 2002), p. 302.

38. See Pliny the Younger, Letter 10.96.

They repeated after me an invocation to the gods, and offered religious
rites with wine and incense before your statue (which for that purpose
I had ordered to be brought, together with those of the gods), and even
reviled the name of Christ: whereas there is no forcing, it is said, those
who are really Christians into any of these compliances: I thought it
proper, therefore, to discharge them. Some among those who were
accused by a witness in person at first confessed themselves Christians,
but immediately after denied it.[39]

Provincials who refused and remained steadfast in their faith
faced immediate execution; Roman citizens who did the same were
officially confined as prisoners and sent to Rome for trial.

The examination of Roman law and the required ritual expressions of loyalty to the perpetual god of the Romans helps unlock
both the reasons for Christians' suffering and the enormous pressure
that tempted them to seek for a safe shelter in Judaism.

The reward

Christians had already paid high social, personal and financial
penalties for their confession of faith in Jesus as the eternal Son of
God and great high priest of the eternal covenant (10:32–34). More
suffering was to come, as 10:35–39 indicates. The future must have
seemed bleak, with further exclusion from the safety provided in
their city of residence; hence the writer of the letter describes the
reward.

The inheritance

The writer knew that the reason for their acceptance of the loss of
their property would now provide a solution for their present
situation. They had done so 'with joy' (10:34b). This reaction must
have surprised and puzzled those outside the Christian faith, given

---

39. Ibid., 10.96.

the importance of the home (the seizure of property was a heavy penalty under Roman law, see p. 151). They had reacted this way because, as the writer says, 'you knew that you yourselves had a better possession and an abiding one' (10:34c, ESV). So he exhorts them not to make the worst decision of their lives now by 'throwing away our confidence, which has a great reward' (10:35).

The endurance

The writer knows that the road immediately ahead will be difficult: 'For you have need of endurance [*hypomonē*]' (10:36, ESV). This word referred to the capacity to hold on in adverse circumstances, survive and even thrive. For example, it was used to describe a tree surviving in adverse conditions such as growing on a rocky cliff face.[40] Remembering that there was a 'great reward' in the future has to be the incentive for still enduring 'in order that you may do the will of God and receive what is promised' (10:35–36).

The remedy the writer prescribes was not only the anticipation of the 'great reward' but also the eschatological promise that there was an end in sight (see e.g., 10:37). The view of the immanent messianic return was in direct opposition to the first-century philosophical view of the eternity of the world.[41] These Christians were facing two choices: continue to live in the light of the promised return of Christ ('and my righteous one shall live by faith', 10:38), or cut and run because they could not face any more adversity. If they retreat from the faith now, God will also retreat from them ('if he shrinks back, my soul will have no pleasure in him', 10:37–38). The writer then hastens to add, 'and we ourselves [*hēmeis*] are not those who shrink back for destruction'. His use of the term 'destruction' indicates how dire the future could be, so he again affirms, 'but [*alla*] we are those who have faith and preserve [our] souls' (10:39).

The writer continues to encourage the Christians to persevere. Firstly he provides a definition of the 'faith' they have: 'the assurance

---

40. Theophrastus, *De causis plantarum* 5.16.3.
41. Cf. Philo's treatise, *The Eternity of the World*.

of things hoped for, the certainty of things not seen' (11:1). He then introduces a 'homily' on what perseverance meant for the righteous from the past who lived by faith, even in times of great adversity. These he designates as 'so great a cloud of witnesses' (12:1).

The race

All examples are part of the writer's remedy to fortify the Christians to lay aside 'every *onkos*', a term that refers to 'weight' or, when used metaphorically, to a 'trouble' that weighs a person down (see *LS*). In this case it is the burden of adverse external circumstances, i.e., the potential further suffering of Christians. They must also shed 'sin that clings so closely'. Just as an athlete discarded his clothes so that he could run his race unencumbered,[42] so too Christians must cast aside the two impediments that will hinder running on the track of the Christian life that could lead through isolated and hostile territory. Participants in ancient Greek marathons had to stay the arduous course, so too Christians 'must run with endurance' in order to finish the race (12:1). The term 'endurance' was previously used in 10:36 where comparable sufferings had to be 'endured', difficult as that was (10:32).

Total focus on the finishing line in athletics was essential. It also was so for Christians who must 'look to Jesus'. The verb (*aphoraō*) means 'to focus without distraction on a distant object'. The way an athlete focused on the ultimate goal illustrates how Christians are to run the race of life without being distracted (12:1). Jesus' focus provides their focus. Knowing the ultimate joy awaiting him, Jesus poured scorn on the humiliating shame of death experienced by crucifixion. He did this as 'the founder and perfecter of our faith' (the latter term was used of the one who brings something to a

---

42. The abandoning of the loincloth in athletics enabled runners to participate unencumbered. Pausanius 1.44.1 attributes this originally to Orsippos at the Olympic Games in 720 BC who 'intentionally let the loincloth slip off him, realizing that a naked man can run more easily than one with it on'. For a discussion of other ancient sources that attribute this convention to others see Newby, *Athletics*, pp. 71–72.

successful conclusion). He also looked beyond his crucifixion knowing he would secure his inheritance, i.e., the place of permanent honour and power at the right hand of God (12:2).

The Christians' previous focus on the future had resulted in their joyful response when they originally suffered great loss with the confiscation of their property (10:34–35). It parallels the 'joy' that Jesus anticipated which enabled him to endure. However the writer, aware of their fragility, admonishes these Christians not to grow weary or fainthearted in running this spiritual race. Their present struggle against sin is certainly not comparable to that of Jesus because they 'have not yet resisted to the point of shedding your blood' (12: 4, ESV).

The exhortation

The quotation from Proverbs 3:11–12 at Hebrews 12:5 is significant because it establishes that the Christians' suffering is not a sign of divine disapproval but the assurance of a divine filial relationship.[43] They must take care that they respond positively to the exhortation to endure this suffering as 'discipline'. Although painful, they are exhorted to see it is as beneficial because it is part of their sanctification that will yield 'the peaceful fruit of righteousness to those who are trained by it' (12:7–11, ESV).

It is also significant that the theme of the shared suffering in identical circumstances is again discussed in 13:3. Lest these Christians forget their past plight in prison, here attention is drawn to the empathy that grew out of their adversity, with an exhortation 'to remember those who are in prison, as though in prison with them; and those who are ill-treated, since you are in the body' (cf. 10:34). O'Brien comments that the 'unusual' phrase 'in the body' 'is

---

43. Suffering or adversity was not seen in this way in the first century. Liebeschuetz notes that 'there is abundant evidence that the Romans were even obsessively convinced of the need to placate the gods' when faced with either. J. H. W. G. Liebeschuetz, *Continuity and Change in Roman Religion* (Oxford: Clarendon Press, 1979), p. 3.

intended to convey the notion of intense identification with those who are suffering'.[44] This letter ends with the good news of Timothy's release from prison, so others who have shared the same experience will undoubtedly rejoice on learning of his release from the suffering of internment (13:23).

The extended discussion of suffering in Hebrews 10:32 – 12:13 concludes with a final exhortation to these Christians to take responsibility, pull themselves together and run on the right track: 'therefore [*dio*] lifting up your drooping hands and strengthening your knees you must make straight paths for your feet in order that what is lame may not be put out of joint but rather be healed' (12:12–13). Those who feel downhearted and disorientated because of their suffering are called upon to get themselves back on track and endure as they run their race. As Attridge notes of this whole section on suffering, 'The exhortation to faithful endurance built on athletic imagery and the proverbial understanding of suffering as educative discipline thus closes on a positive note.'[45]

Finally, the writer appeals to them to 'bear with my word of exhortation' which is how he designates his letter (13:22). The bottom line is about persevering in suffering as the response to what Mitchell describes as 'the overwhelming pressure to conform imposed by the institutions of his city and the activities of his neighbours' to venerate the alternative eternal divinity and high priest.[46] The punishment pending is described as 'suffering outside the camp', the very difficult and lonely path of exile, where they must go as Jesus did and experience his presence (13:12–13).

In conclusion this 'word of exhortation' aims to keep these Christians running the race while enduring ongoing suffering because

---

44. P. T. O'Brien, *The Letter to the Hebrews* (Grand Rapids: Eerdmans; Nottingham: Apollos, 2010), p. 508.

45. H. W. Attridge, *The Epistle to the Hebrews: A Commentary on the Epistle to the Hebrews* (Hermeneia; Philadelphia: Fortress, 1989), p. 365.

46. Mitchell, *Anatolia*, vol. 2, p. 10.

of the lasting prize at the finishing line.[47] They must not yield to the alternative option of rejecting the one who alone possesses eternal divinity and gives a lasting reward to those who finish the race. In the meantime, it is Jesus who provides the ongoing support they need to endure suffering. He is the true, faithful, empathetic and active great high priest who shows mercy and gives grace to help in a needy time such as this (4:16).

---

47. Prizes for races won at the Games at Olympia and Delpi were 'simple crowns of vegetation', crowns of celery in Isthmia, and monetary rewards in the Capitoline Games instituted in AD 86 where winners were given 'a simple wreath, apparently of oak leaves', Newby, *Athletics*, pp. 37, 41.

INDEX OF SCRIPTURE REFERENCES

discover more great Christian books
at www.ivpbooks.com

Full details of all the books from Inter-Varsity Press – including reader reviews, author information, videos and free downloads – are available on our website at **www.ivpbooks.com**.

IVP publishes a wide range of books on various subjects including:

Biography

Christian Living

Bible Studies

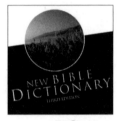

Reference

Commentaries

Theology

On the website you can also sign up for regular email newsletters, tell others what you think about books you have read by posting reviews, and locate your nearest Christian bookshop using the *Find a Store* feature.

IVP publishes Christian books that are **true to the Bible** and that **communicate the gospel, develop discipleship** and **strengthen the church** for its mission in the world.